Betsey Lewis

The GALACTIC KNOWING

Visions of the Future

THE GALACTIC KNOWING

Visions of the Future

Betsey Lewis

Book Titles by Betsey Lewis

Alaska's Deadly Triangle
Prophecy Now
Signals from Heaven
Lizzie Extraterrestrials Worldwide
Prophecy 2022 and Beyond
Stargates
Extraterrestrial Encounters of The Extraordinary Kind
Star Beings
Déjà vu
Ancient Serpent Gods
Mystic Revelations of Seven
Mystic Revelations of Thirteen
Earth Energy: Return to Ancient Wisdom
Communicating with the Other Side
Angels, Aliens, and Prophecy II

More books by Betsey on Amazon

Spiritual Books for Children
Alexander Phoenix
The Story of Rainbow Eyes
A Worm Named Sherm

The Galactic Knowing: Visions of the Future

ISBN: 979-8853661769

Cover design by Betsey Lewis
(12/4)

When the red star of Regulus aligns just before dawn in the gaze of the Sphinx, a new knowledge shall come into the world. — The Lady of Light prophecy in the book, *UFO of GOD,* by Chris Bledsoe

Betsey Lewis

CONTENT

CHAPTER ONE
PAST VISIONS

There are those who are feeling the stirring of megalithic changes coming to Earth. The Awakened Ones already know what is to come—they have been given warnings through lucid dreams and from Star Beings. It is time for humanity to open its third eye and heart chakras and see what is coming in these critical times. Listen and heed the directives of spirit that contain the wisdom you need. Ancient words of wisdom have stood eternal and pure since they were first given, and now it is up to us to decipher their prophecies.

There are skeptics who have labeled me a "fake psychic"—whatever that means. This will clarify my visions and precognitive dreams, and the clairvoyance that I call the "Knowing" that something is going to happen before it happens.

I am a third-generation psychic and there are probably more psychics in my ancestry still uncovered. My mom and my paternal great-aunt had the gift of foresight. Mom could bi-locate and be at two places at the same time, communicate by telepathy, and recall a past life in China as a male laborer for the Great Wall of China. She even recalled being buried inside the wall or near it when she died in China. My great aunt Grace was intuitive and spoke to the spirit of her brother, my grandfather after he passed. My grandfather appeared to me shortly after he died in 1958 and saved my life two months later.

My first UFO encounter happened in 1950 when I was eight months old. Of course, I didn't recall it until 1981 after undergoing hypnosis.

My parents attended the University of Idaho in Moscow in 1950 when I entered the world under the astrological sign of Pisces at 7:48 a.m. A small number of people are born with a rare formation in their astrology charts called a Yod, also known as the "*Finger of God*" or "*Finger of Fate.*" There are two Yods in my birth chart which means I have a unique spiritual assignment in life. The musician Prince had two Yods in his natal chart and Princess Diana and both of her sons, William and Harry, have birth charts with Yods.

During the 1930s, my great-grandmother Kathryn Bollerman traveled the world and stopped in Israel to see the Holy Land and while visiting sacred places, she collected water from the Jordan River and brought it back to the United States. The Bible says Jesus was baptized in the Jordan River by John the Baptist. Although my Great Grandmother Kathryn never lived to see me born, dying in 1946, she asked that the Holy water be used to christen her first-born great-grandchild in the Catholic Church. I was christened by the holy water of Jordan.

The total of my birthdate is seven, a spiritual number mentioned 635 times in the Bible. Seven represents the realm of "divine vibration." It is the enlightened power of the chakra energies. There are seven colors in the rainbow. Seven continents on Earth. Seven days to a week and seven notes to the diatonic scale. There are the seven seals covered in

Revelation before Armageddon. Seven trumpets will sound before the end of the world.

The Battle of Jericho described in the Bible was the first battle fought by the Israelites in the course of the conquest of Canaan. According to Joshua 6:1:27, the walls of Jericho fell after the Israelites marched around the city walls once a day for six days, seven times on the seventh day, with the priests blowing their horns daily and the people shouting.

There are theories that the vibration of the marching and priests blowing their horns for seven days brought the walls of Jericho down with resonance. Seven is that powerful!

Mom attended art class and Dad enrolled in an engineering class. By October I was seven months old, and my parents decided to visit southern Idaho, usually an eight-hour drive, to introduce their first-born grandchild to grandparents and family. I was to be christened at that time by Holy Water brought back from Israel by my great-grandmother.

My first UFO encounter: It was night, nearly ten o'clock when we reached the small farming community of New Meadows. Not one car had passed on the two-lane highway. Another mile later, a roar engulfed the car, shaking it like a toy. Fearing a plane had engineer problems and was going to crash, Dad pulled to the side of the road, jumped out of the car, and scanned the sky for a plane. There was nothing there except stars and the roar was gone instantly. Only the sounds of crickets permeated the night. Meanwhile, I slept peacefully inside a wicker basket placed on the car's back seat.

What could have caused the intense roar that stopped so abruptly? Still puzzled by the roar, my parents continued to Southern Idaho, feeling as if more had happened.

The same story was told to me by my parents through the years, but that all changed in 1980 when my uncle Martin added a twist to my parents' frightening roar after he recalled the 1975 television movie, *The UFO Incident*, on Betty and Barney Hill's UFO encounter and abduction by small gray aliens on September 19, 1961. They claimed to be abducted by a "flying saucer" that stopped their car in a rural portion of the state of New Hampshire and small gray aliens took them aboard their spacecraft to be examined. The incident became known as the "Hill Abduction" and the "Zeta Reticuli Incident" because two ufologists connected the star map shown to Betty Hill by the alien leader in the region known as the Zeta Reticuli system. Their story was adapted into the 1966 best-selling book, *The Interrupted Journey,* and a subsequent 1975 television film.

My paternal grandparents feared my parents and I had been involved in a car accident, arriving in Twin Falls two hours late. My dad had driven from Moscow. Idaho to Twin Falls many times, knowing how long the drive would take. At the time, my parents had not explanation for their missing time. Mom had frightening nightmares that I was kidnapped during the New Meadows incident.

July 1947 started the big UFO flap after a "flying saucer" crash outside of Roswell, New Mexico, where the military recovered extraterrestrials bodies. Of course, the military denied it shortly after claiming it was a crashed saucer. People everywhere were reporting strange saucer-shaped craft from 1947 into the 1950s. There were reports of disk-shaped craft hovering over cars, causing them to stall. Whether these stories were true, I can't say, but they were in the news.

After hearing that my parents lost two hours in time and couldn't account for the missing time, I wrote a letter to renowned New York UFO investigator Budd Hopkins who replied and referred me to MUFON Investigator and best-selling author Ann Druffel in Los Angeles where Mom and I lived in 1980.

Mom's hypnosis session was scheduled for September of 1980. Ann Druffel and her assistant Vincent arrived at Mom's apartment in the evening hours, and I left with a friend not wanting to hear what Mom said that might influence my regression session. Ann explained that even though I was seven or eight months old at the time of the incident, everything we have ever experienced remains in our memory bank. Nobody ever forgets anything. Everything that we pass through in our lifetime makes an impression that is stored away in our brains. Hypnosis can unlock forgotten memories.

My session was in February of 1981. During my regression, I described us on the road, alone in the darkness of night, being pulled up into a huge spacecraft where small beings with huge black eyes and oversized heads awaited us. I described the spindly alien beings with light radiating from their heads. A few days later, we reviewed the taped sessions and were shocked by the similarities in our stories. Some of the information Mom recalled was new to me. Mom sobbed during part of the session, the fear permeated her voice as she visualized something large hovering in the sky that frightened her, and a strange green smell. Something wanted to abduct me, she sensed.

More of my regression revealed that we were pulled up into a huge spacecraft and examined by gray beings. The floor was transparent. Dad was sitting in a cup-shaped chair staring into outer space on the floor below me, and mom was trapped inside a clear tube calling out for me. After we were examined, the ETs placed us back into the car. Dad was slumped over the wheel as if asleep, but Mom appeared asleep too.

Did my parents and I encounter a UFO in 1950 and were we abducted and examined by small gray aliens? I can't say for sure, but I sense it was a real encounter. Two hours passed during our weekend trip and there was no explanation for the missing time and the car shaking from a roar in the sky except a UFO hovering over our car and an abduction.

By the age of three, I began describing to my mother two small spirit entities. And calling them by name "Peak-a-boo" and "Patay." Mom sensed they were guardian angels, but maybe they were extraterrestrials.

My second UFO encounter took place at age seven as I walked home four blocks from my first-grade class in Twin Falls. That September day was overcast but I sensed something watching me through the clouds. As I looked up a massive silver object hovered above me. My instinct told me to run and hide so I ducked into some bushes, and unexpectedly I was crossing a busy street, but I don't remember how. Mom always warned me about crossing busy streets. The first home I found I began knocking frantically on the door, waiting for someone to answer. The door was unlocked, so I entered and found a bedroom, hiding under the bed. The whole event seemed surreal, like a dream. Did I really cross a busy street to hide under a bed when home was so much closer?

Mom was frantic when I finally arrived home nearly an hour late. I told her about my silver disk in the sky that followed me and how I hid in someone's house for a while. I had no idea one hour had passed.

We walked around the neighborhood as other children also witnessed a "giant silver disc or saucer" in the sky but it was never in the newspaper or television. An elderly woman suggested it was some experimental military aircraft.

A few days later recurring visions of catastrophic Earth changes began to haunt my nightly dreams. In all my dreams I was an adult escaping tsunami waves, erupting volcanoes, earthquakes, and violent winds. Others were escaping the erupting earthquakes and seismic activity happening worldwide. I was given these prophetic visions/dreams of a future event involving the entire planet.

On December 1, 1957, my beloved paternal grandfather Fred passed away from a massive heart attack. Days later, his white gauzy apparition stood beside my bed late one night staring down at me. I didn't recognize his youthful appearance and his misty image. Too frightened to scream out, I dove under the bed covers and didn't surface until dawn.

A month later, snow fell for two days, piling up on our country road. Because we lived on a rural road it wasn't plowed as often as city streets. On the third day, a big snowbank was left on the east side of the road. That day my sister stayed at a friend's house, so I made a snow cave on the side of the road and dug deep into the heavy wet snow, crawling inside. Instantly, the entire snow cave collapsed, trapping me inside as I gasped for air, unable to move in the dark icy cave. I was going to die, buried alive and no one would find me right away. I prayed in my mind, and suddenly a hand pulled me from the snowbank.

Dazed, I stood beside the snowbank covered in snow and turned to thank my rescuer, but no one was there. An invisible presence pulled me from the heavy snowbank, and I knew it was Grandfather Fred. I was too embarrassed to tell Mom about my near-death incident.

Through the years my life has been saved from car accidents, my dad's violent temper against Mom and me, several major surgeries, hemorrhaging from a botched surgery, a violent boyfriend who tried to choke me to death, and severe asthma attacks.

At the age of twelve, I began giving psychic readings to Mom's friends. My sister Kathy and I were sent to live with our great Aunt Grace in Hollywood for the school year in 1966. I had a crush on Mark Lindsay (yes, I was a teen groupie), lead singer with Paul Revere and the Raider band who had played at my parent's lake resort seven miles from Twin Falls in 1962. They also performed at the local Twin Falls National Guard Armory in the early 1960s.

While in Los Angeles, a schoolmate who knew Mark Lindsay gave me his address at 10050 Cielo Drive in Benedict Canyon, Beverly Hills. A friend drove me to Mark's house on Saturday afternoon. I rang the buzzer on the gate and was greeted by Charles, the elderly black caretaker, who gave me a tour of the house while Mark and his roommate record producer Terry Melcher, Doris Day's son, were out of town.

10050 Cielo Drive house

The house sat on a hillside with lots of bushes and brilliant white and red flowers. It was a lovely cottage on the outside, but inside I felt ill as a creepy, ominous feeling engulfed me. Something evil lurked there. I left immediately, unable to shake the palpable darkness the hung inside the house. Before 1969, Mark Lindsay and Terry Melcher had moved out of the house.

In February 1969, Sharon Tate and her husband Roman Polanski rented the Cielo home. On August 8, 1969, four of Charles Manson's cult followers entered the house now owned by film producer Roman Polanski and his 26-year-old actress wife Sharon Tate, who was 8 ½ months pregnant at the time. Tex Watson and three of the Manson cult women killed Sharon Tate, her friend hairstylist Jay Sebring, Polanski's 32-year-old friend, Wojciech Frykowski, and his twenty-five-year-old girl friend heiress to the Folder's fortune, Abigail Folger, the caretake William Garret, 19-years-old, and his friend Steven Parent, only 18 years old. Polanski was in Europe at the time filming a new movie. Music producer Quincy Jones was Jay Sebring's friend and was invited to the party that night but didn't attend.

The people were massacred in the house on the order of crazed Charles Manson. Reports claimed Manson was looking for record producer Terry Melcher, who was instrumental in shaping the mid-to-late 1960s California Sound and folk-rock movements. Others believe Manson knew that Melcher was gone but was still angered by his rejection. Manson always believed he was destined to be a big rock star and had written several songs he believed the Beach Boys would record or that Melcher could help make his dream come true. The house was rumored to be haunted by Sharon Tate's ghost. Another house was built further away from the Cielo Drive residence, and the original house was demolished in 1994, and replaced by an 18,000-square-foot Mediterranean-style spec house nicknamed "Villa Bella." The 9-bedroom, 13-bathroom megamansion.

Psychics visiting the hillside home claimed there was an evil presence there before Sharon Tate and her friends were murdered. Walking through the dark foreboding house three years earlier haunted me for years. I knew something evil was going to happen there.

In the fall of 1967, Mom and I boarded a Greyhound bus in Twin Falls, with only two suitcases and one-hundred dollars, and moved to Los Angeles with no prospects of jobs or a place to live. We trusted our lives were being guided. Sympathetic people let us stay at their Santa Monica home until we could afford an apartment and soon, we were hired at the same Union Bank in downtown Los Angeles. I worked in new accounts and Mom worked in the Analysis Department.

We moved into a nice apartment on Sixth Street off of mid-Wilshire, a few blocks from the famous Ambassador Hotel. In May, I began to experience lucid dreams. In one eerie dream, a gypsy drew a cross on my right palm with her long fingernails, causing blood to drip from my hand. The dream was symbolic, but of what? Was a martyr going to die soon? The answer was yes.

Robert Kennedy, a presidential candidate, was in town speaking at the Ambassador Hotel on June 5, 1968. At 12:15 a.m., Mom and I woke to hear ambulances and police sirens blaring and red lights flashing. We switched on the radio and heard that Robert F. Kennedy had been shot several times in the head and rushed to the Good Samaritan Hospital. Robert Kennedy was the martyr in my strange symbolic dream on the bloody cross and now the dreams of millions of people had been vanquished like Robert's brother, John F. Kennedy. Robert Kennedy died the next day, June 6, 1968.

By 1971, I was employed at a brokerage firm in Beverly Hills and had to be there by five in the morning. On the morning of February 6, I dreamt of a huge earthquake in Los Angeles and felt my mom and I would be safe. The same earthquake dream continued each morning for two more days. Then on February 9, 1971, there was no dream, but I was dressed and ready to catch the bus before six. At 6:01 a.m. PST, the earth shook, and our apartment swayed back and forth. Mom had already taken the bus and I was ready to walk out the door. Thankfully, there was only minor damage to our apartment.

The 6.6 magnitude earthquake epicenter occurred near Magic Mountain, about six miles northeast of Sylmar, at a depth of about seven miles. The damage was extensive in Sylmar, and many roadway failures and the partial collapse of several major freeway interchanges. As I rode the bus to my job, I noticed some high-rise buildings damaged with windows completely blown out. An underground parking garage in Beverly Hills on Wilshire Boulevard was flooded. The earthquake caused $500 million in damage and killed sixty-four people.

By 1972, I was working at CBS News on Sunset Boulevard near Vine in the traffic department and a few months later I worked for the department head of sales. Mom continued to work at a bank in Beverly Hills. One day while I was in the restroom at CBS, a reporter came in. She had given a report on air about the death of Robert Kennedy, and she was at the Ambassador Hotel a few feet from Kennedy. I asked her what she had seen, sensing that she hadn't told the whole story.

She said there were many people in the kitchen area trying to get out as another man stepped up and shot Kennedy from behind. It wasn't Sirhan Sirhan, she said emphatically. I asked her why she didn't notify the authorities about the other man, and she replied, "Are you kidding? I don't have a death wish." I asked what she meant. "I don't want to become another mysterious death like the ones who witnessed President John Kennedy's assassination in Dallas."

Today, Robert F. Kennedy, Jr. to this day believes Sirhan Sirhan did not kill his father, and although many say the RFK Jr. is a conspiracy theorist, he's right that his father was shot by someone else—and it wasn't Sirhan Sirhan.

Through the years I have been shown visions of the future that came true. One year before the Trade Towers in New York City were hit by planes on 9-11-2001 I had a scary dream the year before. In my dream, there was a giant apple tree filled with apples and covered in green leaves. Suddenly the apples and leaves began to fall, and then the entire tree was sucked into the ground and vanished. I woke up in a terrifying sweat.

One year later, on September 11, 2001, the New York City Trade Tower buildings were hit by planes and collapsed killing 2,977 people. My dream indicated the buildings were rigged with explosives, causing the buildings to implode like a demolition project. My dream of a giant apple tree symbolically represented New York City, known as the "Big Apple."

In March 2011 there were unsettling news reports of strange fish and dolphin behavior in the Pacific Ocean.

Swarms of fish and dolphins were seen off the coast of California. This was a sign of a major earthquake in the Pacific.

On March 11, 2011, an undersea 9.0 megathrust earthquake occurred in the Pacific Ocean, 72 km east of the Oshika Peninsula in Japan. The quake lasted approximately six minutes, causing a tsunami that killed 19,759 people.

On December 14, 2012, I woke at 6 a.m. Mountain time with the strangest feeling of dread, knowing something horrible was going to happen that day. A little over an hour later at 9:30 am Eastern time, 20-year-old Adam Lanza walked into the Sandy Hook Elementary School and shot and killed 26 people. Twenty of the dead were young children.

In June of 2016, I had a powerful vision of Donald Trump dressed in a long black overcoat taking the oath of office as President of the United States on Friday, January 20, 2017. I saw Melania Trump wearing a light-color coat. She wore a light blue coat on that day. While other psychics predicted Hillary Clinton as the next President, I was one of the few psychics to accurately predict Trump's win. My prediction was posted on the NewsMax website:

https://www.newsmax.com/Headline/Psychics-divided-Election/2016/11/05/id/757228/

I predicted Prince Harry and Meghan would wed and have two children—a boy and a girl. January 2021, I predicted Queen Elizabeth's husband, Prince Philip, would pass soon. He died on April 9, 2021. Next, I had a vision of Queen Elizabeth following him in death before the end of 2022. Queen Elizabeth passed on my daughter's birthday, September 8, 2022.

In 2021 as COVID was raging, I was warned not to get the COVID vaccine, and in my last prophecy book, *Prophecy Now*, I also warned people who received the COVID vaccines and boosters would suffer from horrible side effects, and that came true. People began to get blood clots and myocarditis. I've seen what the vaccines have done to family, and how one close relative died from a blood clot shortly after getting the vaccine. People have experienced adverse reactions and even death. I can't even imagine what will happen to infants and children vaccinated at such young ages and how they will suffer all kinds of ailments from the vaccines as they grow. We've seen what has happened to some celebrities. Dr. Aseem Malhotra, a National Health Service (NHS) trained cardiologist, looked into evidence on COVID-19 vaccines, specifically the mRNA vaccines after his father passed away suddenly after receiving the Pfizer vaccine. He felt that his father's rapidly progressive coronary artery disease and sudden cardiac arrest were most likely due to the mRNA product.

I'll even go a step further and say that one day it will be discovered that the COVID-19 vaccine altered DNA.

People who still speak out about it and their horrible side effects are censored. That says a lot when people can't speak freely about something, which means something is wrong if something is hidden from the public.

In 2023, pharmaceutical companies are still pushing the vaccines and boosters. COVID-19 has mutated so much it isn't the killer it once was, and these vaccines won't help. We know that flu vaccines never seem to work as the flu mutates every year.

I also predicted that former President Trump would never be impeached, and that came true when the Senate acquitted him twice.

Here's how my guardian angels prevented a head-on car collision on the day before my husband and I were to be wed in Tahoe, California. Instead of flying to Tahoe, we decided to take turns driving. A long-time friend joined.

An inner voice, "the Knowing," told me to drive first. We took a route we had never taken before on Highway 95 from Boise, Idaho through Jordan, Valley, Oregon, a busy two-lane highway without rest stops or any place to pull off the road. Huge semi-trucks passed us carrying modular homes, making it impossible to pass.

As we passed Jordan Valley, 62 miles from Boise, an older model car suddenly swerved into our lane, headed directly for our car, traveling at 65 mph or faster. Time seemed to slow down, it was as if someone took control of the steering wheel, and a wave of peace engulfed me. I removed my foot from the gas pedal and steered as far as possible to the right-hand side of the road without going into a deep embankment.

According to my husband, who sat in the back seat behind me, the car missed us by inches and then continued down the wrong side of the road until it vanished around a curve. I prayed that no one would be hit by a confused or drunk driver. None of our cell phones worked in the area or we would have called the police. If the car had hit us, I'm sure my husband and I would have died instantly from the impact, and my friend severely injured in the front passenger seat.

Once we reached Winnemucca, Nevada, I called the Jordan police department and told them about the near-car accident. There were no accidents reported on the road that day. My angels saved our lives that day and we had a beautiful wedding day in April in Lake Tahoe with close friends and family.

On September 27, 2023, I gave this prophetic warning on my Earth News blog: *In the past two days, brilliant red auroras have appeared over Europe like they did in 1938 before World War II. Are we being warned of a great conflagration? My answer is a definite YES!* Red auroras are rare. Typically, the famous Northern Lights are made up of predominantly green hues, and while flashes or streaks of crimson are sometimes seen, sustained red skies are extremely uncommon.

On October 7, 2023, Hamas broke through Israeli fences and killed 1,400 innocent Israeli men, women and children. The red aurora warned of this coming war.

****

To those who doubt my gift, I have no words. My word is my truth. My life has not been easy, but I've always felt my mission was to help others with my psychic gift. My parents fought all the time and often my sister and I were pulled out of school and on the run from my father's abuse. As an adult, I was homeless for two months, living in a tent in the mountains of Idaho as snow fell. I was nearly killed by an abusive alcoholic boyfriend, and I have had two major surgeries that nearly cost me my life. These experiences made me more empathetic to others and their life's problems.

Like all psychics, I have misses. There isn't one psychic in the world who is one hundred percent accurate—not even the sixteenth-century astrologer Nostradamus or the late Edgar Cayce, known as the "Sleeping Prophet". Scholars are still trying to decipher Nostradamus quatrains.

If such an infallible psychic existed in the world, they'd be working for a top-secret government agency, and never see the light of day. All psychics are fallible.

Most believe that all events are set in some predetermined future that can't be changed, but that's a false belief. The future is constantly changing. It is malleable and can be altered by human interaction and mass consciousness. Humans can alter some future events by creating a negative Prime Event like 9-11 or they can create a positive Prime Event like the Harmonic Convergence, the world's first synchronized global peace meditation that occurred on August 16-17, 1987, organized by José Argüelles before the internet existed.

People all over the world gathered in sacred places and power points like Mount Shasta to meditate. According to Argüelles, the Harmonic Convergence also began the final 25-year countdown to the end of the Mayan Long Count in 2012, which would be the so-called end of history and the beginning of a new 5,125-year cycle. The evils of the world (war, materialism, violence, abuses, injustice, oppression) would end with the birth of the 6th Sun and the 5th Earth on December 21, 2012.

Peace did not encompass the world as José predicted, but he had faith his world meditation would change the course of history and bring down the Berlin Wall. It happened on November 9, 1989, two years after the Harmonic Convergence.

On 12-12-2009, I interviewed Dr. Jose Arguelles in Australia on my Rainbow Vision Network. This amazing man passed in 2011, at age 72. Since 2009, four thousand, three hundred people have listened to his words on my YouTube channel: https://www.youtube.com/watch?v=bIH2TPx8N-Y

Isaiah 2:19: When the Lord stands up from His throne to shake up the earth, His enemies will crawl with fear into the holes in the rocks and into the caves, because of the glory of His majesty!

CHAPTER TWO

THE STARS FELL

Should we take the ancient prophecies literally or symbolically? The first four judgments in Revelations are focused on Earth and its inhabitants, then the last three are more cosmic expressions. This speaks to their nature and purpose. Remember, God promised that the Earth would never be destroyed by water again. Does that mean by fire—nuclear fire?

Peter 3:12: *Waiting for and hastening the coming of the day of God, because of which the heavens will be set on fire and dissolved, and the heavenly bodies will melt as they burn!*

We live in precarious times where six countries—China, France, Russia, North Korea, the United Kingdom, Israel, and the United States hold nuclear weapons. Soon Iran will have that capability. All it would take is one nuclear missile fired to start a holocaust of unimaginable proportions.

It appears that President Biden wants war...a world war. President Biden wants China and Russia to see that we have a bomb 24 times more powerful than the one that was dropped on Hiroshima, Japan in World War II. Looks like we haven't stopped testing nukes underground. What insanity. Do world leaders want to annihilate the world's population and the Earth? It appears that way.

A fact sheet included with the release said the B61-13 will have a similar yield to the B61-7, which according to a Defense News report, has a maximum yield of 360 kilotons. The load is 24 times larger than the bomb dropped on Hiroshima, Japan, during World War II, which was about a 15-kiloton bomb. The B61-13 would also be about 14 times larger than the bomb dropped on Nagasaki, which was 25 kilotons.

The announcement comes amid rising tensions around the globe, with the U.S. conducting a high-explosive experiment at a nuclear test site in Nevada earlier this month. Corey Hinderstein, the deputy administrator for defense nuclear nonproliferation at the National Nuclear Security Administration, said the test was meant to advance "our efforts to develop new technology in support of U.S. nuclear nonproliferation goals. They will help reduce global nuclear threats by improving the detection of underground nuclear explosive tests."

The test came as Russia was largely expected to announce it was pulling out of the 1966 Comprehensive Nuclear Test Ban Treaty, which was designed to ban nuclear explosions anywhere in the world. However, the treaty was never ratified by China, India, Pakistan, North Korea, Israel, Iran and Egypt. The U.S. conducted a high-explosive experiment at a nuclear test site in Nevada hours after Russia revoked a ban on atomic weapons testing, which Moscow said would put it on par with the United States.

American officials have said more transparency is needed because while the U.S. and Russia don't test warheads, they do conduct so-called sub-critical experiments—explosions that verify weapon designs without the amount of atomic material needed to sustain a chain reaction, the Bloomberg report said. There are widespread concerns that Russia could resume nuclear tests to try to discourage the West its continued support of Ukraine. Russian President Vladimir Putin has said that while some experts have talked about the need to conduct nuclear tests, he hasn't yet formed an opinion on the issue.

My dear friend Corbin Harney, Spiritual Leader of the Western Shoshone Nation (1920-2007), protested the nuclear testing and uranium mining next to Tribal Land in Nevada in the 1990s. Corbin said, *"Our land is suffering on account of nuclear testing and uranium mining. We have to preserve this Earth. We rely on this Earth to give us food, clothing, and all the luxury that we have. Everything is here for us to use, but nuclear energy is not the way to continue with what we have. We don't understand radiation or how the release of nuclear energy is affecting the Earth. Our forefathers didn't know anything about it, and our medicine people don't know how to cure people from it. What we do here in Nevada affects the life of everyone on the planet."*

There was evidence that the underground tests in Nevada leaked radiation above ground. "Down-winders," people who lived downwind from the Nuclear Test Site, especially those in southern Utah, had extremely high numbers of cancers, leukemia, and other physical deformities in the population.

Asteroid hitting Earth

Through the 4.5 billion years Earth has existed, asteroids large and small have bombarded it. Scientists speculate that an asteroid wiped out the dinosaurs 65 million years ago. If you think we are protected by some invisible barrier, think again! Earth has dodged many asteroid bullets.

The opening of the Sixth Seal portends an event that could rock the entire Earth, such as a shift of the poles.

I looked when He opened the sixth seal, and behold, there was a great earthquake, and the sun became black as sackcloth of hair, and the moon became like blood. And the stars of heaven fell to the earth, as a fig tree drops its late figs when it is shaken by a mighty wind. Then the sky receded as a scroll when it rolled up, and every mountain and island was moved out of its place. And the kings of the earth, the great men, the rich men, the commanders, the mighty men, every slave and every free man, hid themselves in the caves and in the rocks of the mountains. (Revelation 6:12-15).

Most people interpret the opening of the Sixth Seal as something that happened thousands of years ago, but certainly not a warning in our time, the twenty-first century.

Can you imagine the entire Earth reeling and shaking as the poles shift position? Can you imagine three days of darkness on one side of the Earth and light on the other side as the Earth's rotation stops? The North Pole would flip to the South Pole position, and the South Pole would be the North Pole. Hurricane winds would tear across the planet and homes turn to splinters in the winds. Meteorites would rain down from the Heavens, both small and large ones, destroying buildings, houses, and starting fires, and killing millions. Tsunamis as tall as buildings would wash over the land and consume everything along the coasts. Volcanoes would erupt with great fury and the Earth would tremble from huge earthquakes.

This happened to the continent of Atlantis eons ago. Those who survived the Earth shift migrated to other lands worldwide taking their knowledge of science and astronomy. They built megalithic structures and pyramids worldwide that would stand the test of time. Records are sealed beneath those pyramids and will one day be discovered.

The seven angels who were holding the seven trumpets prepared to blow them.

When the first one blew his trumpet, there came hail and fire mixed with blood, which was hurled down to the earth. A third of the land was burned up, along with a third of the trees and all green grass. When the second angel blew his trumpet, something like a large burning mountain was hurled into the sea. A third of the sea turned to blood, and a third of the creatures living in the sea-died, and a third of the ships were wrecked.

When the third angel blew his trumpet, a large star burning like a torch fell from the sky. It fell on a third of the rivers and on the springs of water. The star was called "Wormwood," and a third of all the water turned to wormwood. Many people died from this water, because it was made bitter.

When the fourth angel blew his trumpet, a third of the sun, a third of the moon, and a third of the stars were struck, so that a third of them became dark. The day lost its light for a third of the time, as did the night. Then I looked again and heard an eagle flying high overhead cry out in a loud voice, "Woe! Woe! Woe[*] *to the inhabitants of the earth from the rest of the trumpet blasts that the three angels are about to blow!*

A woman from Washington State sent me this email this year:

Betsey, I woke up from a dream this a.m.: I am in my backyard, I look up in see my home leaning to the north as were the trees, etc. Then I stated, 'Is there an earthquake??' Everything shifted back to normalcy. Then I woke up! I feel there was a major shift in the planet on all levels. I live in Kalama, WA. Did you notice the shift physically? Pray Love Pray Truth Pray Peace Blessings, Karin.

Suddenly people notice two suns in the sky during the morning hours as the sun rises and before sunset. Are they capturing Planet X (Nibiru)? Planet X is a rogue planet known as a brown dwarf or failed star that slings through our solar system every 3,657 years or more. This makes it a planet of our solar system, but one only appearing in ancient records because it seems to disappear into space between passages.

Why does it sling, and not go round and round like Earth and the other planets? Coming out of the Big Bang, when the suns and planets were forming and clumping, Planet X started this sling orbit by going around TWO suns. It slings back and forth past them like a pendulum, and cannot stop this pattern, once started.

Two suns?

Most suns are binaries, dancing around each other in a perpetual dance, but our sun appears to be singular, at least that is what the astrophysicists tell us. This is only because its binary, the second sun in the pair, never lit, and thus as a dark hunk out in space is hidden from view most of the time. Our sun and its binary twin do not have a frenetic dance, but are stationary, which may be one reason the sling orbit of Planet X was able to set in place.

NASA and JPL went looking for Planet X in the early 1980s. This subject came up during the sci.Astro debates in 1998, during a debate with Jim Scotti, an astronomer well known, who works out of the Tucson observatory, famously known as the Pope Scope or LUCIFER because the Pope bought time at the observatory to peer into the southern skies, perhaps looking for Planet X.

Naturally, Jim denied that anyone was looking for the Sun's binary twin, or that during the search they discovered Planet X as a rogue planet slinging past both suns in its pendulum orbit.

Taken in 2023 in Los Angeles, California

CHAPTER THREE

PHOENIX RISING

And the Great Firebird Phoenix was seen rising up from the smoldering ashes deep within the Earth. Its flaming iridescent golden feathers caught the sunlight and reflected blinding beacons out onto the land--the sign of a New Age of Awareness, Eternal Peace, and The Galactic Knowing.

Photographs of what appeared to be a giant flaming-orange bird flying over the Grand Teton National Park might initially be called a hoax or a camera anomaly. The photos appeared in a video uploaded by YouTube's MrMBB333, who keeps an eye on seismic activity worldwide. The bird segment was reportedly taken from an unmanned webcam near Jenny Lake, a glacial lake in Wyoming. Both MrMBB333 and other sites showing the photos refer to it as a "fire" bird or "fiery bird" and naturally try to link it to the flaming Phoenix in Greek and Roman mythology.

The airspace it was spotted in was above the Grand Teton National Park was closed at the time because of a mysterious crack in the ground. A crack that was less than ten miles from Yellowstone National Park, home of the largest super volcano in North America, had been the center of hundreds of recent mini-earthquakes, unusual geyser activity, and the appearance of a flaming golden bird.

It's unclear whether the puzzling giant-bird photo was taken by one of the park's monitoring cameras nor is it clear which came first—the crack or the creature. There don't seem to be any other photos or witnesses. Because its color resembles fire, no one linked it to the Native American legend of the Thunderbird.

According to Mary Summer Rain's Chippewa medicine women mentor "No Eyes" in the book *Phoenix Rising*, she told Mary this: "The great Phoenix is gonna rise up again just like times ago. He's already there. He's been forming for years now. He's ready to break out of Earth Mother's womb. If peoples quiet themselves, they gonna feel the labor contractions of Earth Mother. She is so, so tired. She gonna give up great Phoenix soon."

The Phoenix flies to herald a New Age. And that age would be a renewed world of humans.

Were the recent booms heard underground worldwide in the past several years the great Phoenix struggling to rise again from deep within the Earth? The legend of the Phoenix says it must be purged in fire to rise up from the ashes renewed. It appears that humans are headed for a fiery purge soon that will bring peace and rejuvenation to those left on the planet.

In today's world, humans have forgotten the ancient ways of the indigenous and the healers who could read the signs in the weather, the bugs, ants, and winds, and some could even control the weather by praying for rain. On the morning of December 26, 2004, an undersea megathrust earthquake measuring 9.1 to 9.3 struck off the west coast of northern

Sumatra, Indonesia. The day before, my husband and I noticed that the moon seemed to be too far north. Nothing was reported that the moon was out of place in the sky, but for us it was. Suddenly the waters around the island were sucked out from the inlets and bays. Indigenous people living on an island off the coast noticed this. It was their medicine man who instructed his people to get to higher ground. They did and survived the massive tsunami with waves up to 100 feet high. The tsunami devastated communities along the surrounding coasts of the Indian Ocean, killing an estimated 227,898 people in 14 countries in one of the deadliest natural disasters in recorded history.

Instead of trusting their instincts and intuition, tourists and residents ran into the bay in the sand, devoid of ocean water. Most perished that day.

Marisol Smiley and one of her Angels

CHAPTER FOUR

A STARSEED'S VISIONS

I met this amazing spiritual lady Marisol Smiley on Facebook and discovered she attracts orbs and angels to her. She has photographed orbs in the sky and angels through the years at her northwestern Florida home. Even her small children have witnessed orbs flying in their bedrooms and were frightened of them at first. Her amazing interview can be accessed on Betsey's Stargate Radio Show. https://www.blogtalkradio.com/stargateradio/2023/06/29/marisol-smileys-encounters-with-angelic-beings-and-ets

Marisol's vision of the near future:

"I saw the Earth split as two Earths. I saw people running

away and crying. The heavens appeared like fire and black clouds covered the sun for four days. As I looked down on the Earth I watched as souls were shooting up towards the heavens and I was waiting on a ship with the shining one. We hovered over the Earth till everything became silent. The new Earth was right next to the old and I was helping children get onto the new Earth. They were mostly children. The only adults were the chosen ones. Almost all adults were gone. This vision bothered me so much that I had to post about it.

People get right with whatever it is and prepare. I saw much more but I will hold myself back to not frighten people. It's a lot worse than you realize. There are plans to take your consciousness and soul and sell it to the highest bidders."

Another Marisol's vision: God bless and protect all his Star seeds and all life that have been chosen. Not all are supposed to be saved. This is where I feel the sadness come in. I was shown the Earth, and the devastation was so hard to comprehend that I saw human skulls all burnt and I was standing on top of their bones. A huge yellow construction truck was moving towards me, and I saw clothes stuck to their tires as it got closer. I saw it was human bodies, a mountain of bodies. I was horrified. As I looked, I saw two little girls peeking out and realized it was my granddaughters whom I had not met yet or even realized who was the parent. They were my little girls. They had a look of disparity and looked towards me to assist them. I awakened feeling so sad and cried for a few moments. I called my mom and told her about my vision, and she calmed me by saying, *that God reveals what is coming to his messengers*.

This happened when I was only 22 years old. Being able to see what is to come is a burden. It's hard to sometimes get the visions out of my mind and be in the present. I want you to know it's time! The evil in the world wants to distract us from what we are here to do. Pray for the Earth and all life!

Someone is listening and sees everything! You may not see them, but they see you. The power of your inner self is greater than you realize. So, assist yourself and your family in what is coming to the USA on our soil. They are already here, and they will continue to come. Be vigilant! This has been happening to me since I was five. The vision and the dreams.

Orbs over Marisol's home in Florida

A Mother shares her Daughter's Visions

This prediction appeared on Facebook, and I don't know who wrote it except her name—Danielle. It's very disjointed but I thought it was important to share it.

"My daughter tells me of the messages she is being shown. Of mostly devastation and fire—everything destroyed, and one man they keep. I feel like it will be in my lifetime. Everything that's been happening, has been ramping up in the last weeks more.

She described him, but I can't figure out who it is (Shire?). I don't think it's someone known to me yet or the world. She's been warned and he's not to be trusted. She doesn't feel fear which I'm grateful she doesn't have fear, yet I think she feels purpose."

People are reporting angelic voices that seem to come from the sky, and more people are receiving apocalyptic visions of f fire or major Earth disasters that take place soon. I have seen visions of major events coming, and even World War III as humanity continues to fight over land, religion, slavery, food, power, and anything you can think of. We share such a beautiful and unique planet, yet we want to destroy it. Why can't we grow up and evolve into peace-loving beings?

Earth Mother is hurting from the bombs dropping and the poisons pumped into her. She's a living breathing entity, and there will come a time when she shows her fury at our disregard for her beauty and life-giving abundance in the oceans, the mountains, and the valleys.

The living fire will be unleashed, death hidden, Within the globes horrible frightful. At night by squadron city reduced to dust. The city aflame, the enemy favored. — Nostradamus

CHAPTER FIVE

WORLD WAR THREE

Last year I received an email from a follower about the approaching World War that would destroy the world. Our leaders are so worried about global warming, yet they should be more worried about our capability to destroy the Earth with nuclear and thermonuclear weapons. It would be humanity's insanity to launch nuclear weapons—it's a no-win situation for all sides.

Robert wrote: *Easter Evening April 16, 2017, in Arvada Colorado. My Polish mother-in-law, Maria Kafarska, was in hospice care for 18 months in our home. We brought her over from Warsaw in 2015 when we saw her health was rapidly failing: She survived the Uprising of Warsaw against the Nazis of WWII, Communism under the Soviet Union, and as a slave in an Austrian Labor Camp/Concentration Camp in WWII.*

She gave my wife a very frightening warning. NEVER return to live again in Europe because a Terrifying New War is Coming soon to Europe. The Russian invasion of Ukraine could very easily spread to war all over the European Continent in the coming months transforming into World War III.

I too have sensed a major conflagration that would ignite World War III as Robert's Polish mother-in-law's vision indicated. I predicted this on my Earth News blog on September 27 after two days of intense red auroras seen in Europe and North America. Red auroras are rare. Again, we have free will to change events through prayers and intentions, but it would take masses of people to come together in prayer and reverence to achieve a positive Prime Event.

People must awaken now rather than support the fraudulent intentions of all acts of war. Threats of war and the creation of enemies serve to keep the masses under control by falsely creating fearful emotions. It's not the people under dictators and tyrants who want to fight and die, it's the leaders who want more control, land, and money. Will the many or the few control the world? Will the few succeed with their desperate game plans to separate humans from each other and destroy life? Those who celebrate war have no emotions and feel nothing for the innocent men, women, and children.

War shatters not only the mind but the soul. Each of you must understand the body-mind complex is highly programmable in a disassociated, traumatized state. In the face of traumatic events, a person's consciousness vacates his or her body and is reluctant to return. When humans are disconnected from their conscious will, they become unwitting participants in behavior-modifying manipulations. It's mind control. It breaks the spirit and resolution of the Human.

We have already seen those who want to change history and destroy the past by altering books and destroying statues of previous wars in America. When the lessons of the past are ignored and rewritten, history repeats itself, playing out age-old dramas in different time frames.

Russia, North Korea, and China have nuclear capabilities, and Iran will have that capability in the next two years or sooner. They deny having any weapons of mass destruction (WMD). But they can't be trusted. War with nuclear warheads is a no-win situation. With the heinous attack on Israel by Hamas terrorists on civilians on October 7, 2023, the next World War has begun and will spread across the lands.

Dr. Doom's prophecy

You probably have never heard of Nouriel Roubini, a 64-year-old NYU economics professor and CEO of Roubini Macro Associates, but he is seriously reconsidering whether he wants to continue living in New York. Mostly because he wants to survive. He says, "There's a scenario in which, in the next twelve months, Russia uses tactical nuclear weapons against Ukraine and then they attack NATO and we start a conventional war with Russia. The first nuclear weapon is gonna go to New York. Being in New York is not safe."

This prediction is reminiscent of time traveler John Titor's warning of World War III when he appeared in a blog in the year 2000 and said a war had taken place in his timeline years before 2036. Washington, D.C. was rubble, and the United States Capitol was in Nebraska.

Dr. Doom, as some call Roubini, feels that even if Manhattan manages to avoid nuclear annihilation, there's still the possibility of a natural disaster, like Hurricane Sandy that flooded New York in 2012, but "much, much worse," he told The Post. "In the next 20 years, most of downtown New York is gonna be underwater."

The late prophecy Edgar Cayce foresaw a huge earthquake in New York City.

Dr. Doom first became known 16 years ago, correctly predicting the collapse of the housing market and the emergence of a worldwide recession. His new book, *Mega Threats: Ten Dangerous Trend that Imperil our Future, and How to Survive Them*, list his ominous predictions. This time,

Roubini foresees global devastation everywhere, like a recession at the end of 2022 that will be "long and ugly" to climate change, along with another pandemic worse than COVID's body count.

Roubini believes that World War III has already begun in Europe. The nation's coasts, he said, will soon be flooded. "Florida's gonna be underwater—all of it, not just Miami. Most of the South will be too hot to live in. You'll have drought from Colorado to California and wildfires like crazy all over the West. We'll have a great migration to the Midwest, into Canada. We'll have to take over Canada. Literally."

As in invade Canada. By military force? "I'm not joking," Roubini insisted. "The Canadians are gonna say no but they don't have the army. They have the land and the water, but no army to defend it. Unless they unify with us, everybody's gonna try and take over Canada. They need a well-armed US to protect them, so we'll become the United States of North America just out of necessity. I mean, there was a reason Trump wanted to buy Greenland."

So why, then, doesn't he just retreat to Canada now? "There's plenty of farmland across the border in Canada," he conceded. "But it's not just about growing your own food and having your own cows pasturing and your own water resources. You also need security, because everybody's gonna want to go there. And I've never used a gun in my life."

For all of Roubini's talk about a "nightmare for humanity" and not having much faith that "people will ever listen," there's at least some part of him that believes in a happy ending.

"I think young people are hearing the message," he said. "I'll be dead in 30 years, but they're the ones who really have the most to lose. Hopefully, there'll be a movement, an uprising against what's coming. It doesn't matter whether it's Republicans or Democrats—these threats are much more severe than our petty partisan debates. This is about whether the human species is going to survive and thrive or we're gonna sink."

And if we sink, he said, "we sink together, and we drown together. We're all in the same boat. We can watch the boat fill with water, or we can work together to do something about it."

Will these horrible events happen?

We never dreamed that a virus called COVID-19 would kill three million humans worldwide. We never dreamed our governments would become so tyrannical, but they did because we allowed it. This is the time for all of us to identify destructive negative thoughts and then change them to positive thoughts. Mass consciousness can create miracles, but humans must be willing to come together in thought and prayer, yet we remain more divided than we have ever been. You are here to restore peace and dignity to humanity. It would be a miracle if millions decided to create another Hamonic Convergence again and change the disastrous road we are headed toward.

War is raging in Ukraine now, and although it appears they are winning over Russia, could Putin ultimately use nuclear weapons? It is of the utmost importance that we realize the ramifications of war. It's an unnecessary act and it harms the soul and spiritual evolution. North Korea is threatening again with test missiles off the coast and will invade South Korea, and China is joining forces with Russia. China will attack Taiwan in 2024.

To have peace worldwide, the people of the world must desire peace and be willing to make the vibrations necessary to create it. A Marian apparition and Jesus warned Lucia, the eldest Fatima child, that if humans didn't change, World War II, would take place, and it did. Now rare blood-red auroras appeared in the Northern Hemisphere in September of 2023, a warning of a great conflagration that will ignite World War III.

Earth is currently experiencing a tumultuous transformation of consciousness never recorded before in our history. It is a critical time of changes and cosmic power. In this world, the role each of us plays is entirely of our own making; we write the script and direct the course of action. The horrendous and startling changes sweeping the globe are blatant signs that inner upheavals of immense proportion are transpiring as people worldwide are challenged to confront the curtailing of their freedom. Many are now remembering the possibilities they agreed to explore before they were born.

Unless our collective consciousness returns to a peaceful, spiritual civilization of the Soul, we might become one more on a long list of extinct species that have either destroyed themselves or their planet. These failed soul evolution experiments and world extinctions happen more than you can imagine throughout the galaxy.

Nuclear Warheads

Most of the world has the capability of nuclear warheads. Estimates of Israel's stockpile range between 80 and 400 nuclear warheads, and the country is believed to possess the ability to deliver them in several methods, including by aircraft, as submarine-launched cruise missiles, and via the Jericho series of intermediate to intercontinental range ballistic missiles. Russia has the most confirmed nuclear weapons, with 5,997 nuclear warheads. The United States has 5,244 warheads, China has 410, France has 290, the United Kingdom has 225, and North Korea has 30 warheads.

During the early 1960s, I grew up with the threat of the atomic bomb striking the United States, and in school, we practiced drills for radiation fallout. Of course, that wouldn't have saved us in such an event depending on where the bomb was dropped. Children during an atomic drill were instructed to run home as fast as they could to be with family. I remember doing that several times in the '60s. My father owned a dehydrated food company in Twin Falls, Idaho and we stored food and water in caves outside in the area in preparation for the bomb being dropped on us. It was a scary time.

Back then, we didn't know enough about radiation fallout and what it would do if the A-bomb was dropped in the Western United States. Most experts believed that a low-yield device (about 1 KT) was the most likely. The A-bomb detonated over Hiroshima was a 15-KT device; India's test on

May 11, 1998, was a 60 KT device while most strategic weapons today are over 1,000 KT.

This is what happens from a nuclear blast:

Air Blast: As with a conventional explosive, a nuclear detonation produces a shock wave or air blast wave. The air blast, with its accompanying winds, can damage structures and injure individuals. Individuals can also be injured by falling debris and flying glass shards. The air blast from a 1 KT detonation could cause 50% mortality from flying glass shards to individuals within an approximate radius of 300 yards (275 m). This radius increases to approximately 0.3 miles (590 m) for a 10 KT detonation.

Heat: The second effect would be extreme heat, a fireball, with temperatures up to millions of degrees. The heat from a fireball is sufficient to ignite materials and cause burns far from the fireball, and the associated intense light may cause blindness. The heat from a 1 KT detonation could cause 50% mortality from thermal burns to individuals within an approximate 0.4 miles (610 m) radius.

This radius increases to approximately 1.1 miles (1800 m) for a 10 KT detonation. Shadowing by structures between the fireball and the individual will prevent or reduce heat effects.

Initial Radiation: The initial radiation is produced in the first minute following detonation. The detonation's intense initial pulse produces ionizing radiation that causes intense radiation exposures. The initial radiation pulse from a 1 KT device could cause 50% mortality from radiation exposure, to individuals, without immediate medical intervention, within an approximate ½ mile (790 m) radius. This radius increases to approximately ¾ mile (1200m) for a 10 KT detonation. Individuals in intervening buildings and building basements may receive reduced exposure due to the additional shielding.

Ground Shock: Ground shock is equivalent to a large earthquake, and it would follow the blast. This could cause additional damage to buildings, roads, communications, utilities, and other portions of the infrastructure. The ground shock and air blast would be expected to cause major disruptions in the local infrastructure.

Secondary Radiation: Secondary radiation exposure due to fallout would occur primarily downwind from the blast, but changing weather conditions could spread radioactivity and enlarge the affected area. For a 1 KT device, radiation exposure from fallout within the first hour after the blast could cause 50% mortality from radiation exposure to individuals without medical intervention, for approximately 3.5 miles (5500 m) downwind of the event. This distance increases to approximately 6 miles (9600 m) for a 10 KT detonation. These distances could be greater or smaller, depending on wind and weather conditions. Individuals in intervening buildings and building basements may receive reduced exposure due to the additional shielding.

What do you do if this happens: Stay Inside: Shelter yourself from airborne radioactive particles, in the form of fallout, by staying inside your home or office, unless instructed to do otherwise. Close the windows, turn off the ventilation system, and stay toward the center of the house or building. If there is a basement, go there. Once the initial blast is over, the existing risk will be from airborne radioactivity.

Listen to the Radio: When you learn that a nuclear detonation has occurred turn on your radio to your local emergency-broadcasting network and listen for instructions. Federal, state, and local agencies will be doing everything they can to minimize the hazards and keep you safe.

A battery-powered radio would be good to own if electrical power is out in your neighborhood. Paying careful attention to any instructions given will help you minimize any radiation exposure. Follow Instructions: Your best chance of avoiding exposure is to do what the experts advise. If told to evacuate after the radioactive cloud has passed or gone in another direction do so immediately. Listen for news of the location of the cloud and travel at a right angle away from the cloud. Even if it has already passed, radioactive contamination may have been deposited on the ground.

Seek Help if Needed: If you know or suspect you've been contaminated or received a radiation dose, seek an assistance center, which will be set up as soon as possible. If that hasn't happened yet, go to a fire station or police station located outside the affected area. Look for Symptoms: If you believe you have been directly in the path of the cloud or in the blast zone itself, watch for symptoms of exposure, like nausea, loss of appetite, reddening of the skin, or diarrhea. Seek immediate medical help if symptoms occur. Blood changes can be measured at even moderate exposures and are among the first detectable symptoms. A doctor can test for those changes.

Watch What You Eat: Avoid drinking fresh milk, and water or eating fresh vegetables from the affected area. One of the most common radionuclides found in a nuclear explosion is iodine-131, which is taken up by and can affect the thyroid. The most common pathway for exposure to iodine-131 is through fresh milk and vegetables contaminated with fallout radiation. Wait until the Department of Health announces that produce and dairy products are safe to eat and drink.

God help us that this scenario never happens.

CHAPTER SIX

THE ENIGMA OF CHRIS BLEDSOE

On September 7, 2023, I interviewed an extraordinary man named Chris Bledsoe on Stargate Radio. Chris has the uncanny ability to summon orbs and otherworldly beings at his home in Fayetteville, North Carolina. The people of Fayetteville have witnessed the orb phenomena and so has the History Channel's Beyond Skinwalker Ranch investigative team when they visited his home. They discovered by monitoring his brain waves that Chris goes into a meditative state and contacts the orb beings and they appear in the sky or the nearby woods.

After the events of 9-11-2001, Chris lost his business and was in financial ruin and suffering from a debilitating chronic disease by 2007. His world was crashing down on him. He was on the verge of the unthinkable—suicide.

That same year, fishing along the banks of the Cape Fear River with three co-workers, and his teenage son, Chris walked away from the campsite and in desperation cried out to God for help. Suddenly, a UFO appeared. When he walked back to his friends, he found them dismayed and terrified by the UFO orbs chasing them and how Chris vanished for four hours. Meanwhile, Chris was stunned that he was gone that long. His son Chris Jr. was hysterical after an orb held him down during the four hours.

After that night things began to change—Chris was healed of his Crohn's Disease and his financial situation began to improve.

The first time he met the Lady of Light was in 2012. At first, he experienced an angry bull charging at him, and he was the matador. It galloped as if it were itself an aspect of the wind. Just as he thought he was going to meet his end, the bull jumped over him, knocking him on his back. He saw stars and branches beyond its translucent body as he fell backward.

Lady of Light and Bull painted by Doug Auld.

Chris rolled over on his stomach so he could try to stand up and run. He pushed himself up from the ground to his hands and knees and saw a woman floating in a circle of light. Poised still and silent, she gazed down at him. He then rose to his knees and spent a minute trying to take in what was happening before him.

Chris found himself kneeling within the circle of light emanating from the Lady. She was about the height of Chris's chin and was barefoot. She wore a gleaming robe that was simple and featureless and hung down to her ankles. To Chris, the robe appeared to be an ancient priestess's robes from Roman times, plus long sleeves drooping past her wrists and an unadorned collar. She had blonde hair and the most dazzling blue eyes he had ever seen. He realized that she was only four and a half feet or five feet tall at the most. Her eyes radiated a sense of calm.

She spoke to Chris in his mind. "You know why I'm here."

As she spoke, Chris was in a trance-like state and said missing time and the beings who captured him were all tools she had used. They were guardians she sent to do her bidding. She vowed that if Chris continued his mission, she would protect his family and him, she would allow the orbs to be photographed and would allow him to show these phenomena to witnesses outside of his family. If he promised to continue talking about the things he witnessed, she'd never leave his side.

For long portions of her disclosure, she raised her pointer finger to her lips as though she were telling Chris to keep a secret or be quiet. He didn't understand what she was saying. Later she told Chris that he would understand when the time was right.

Before the Lady had entered his life, he had been given a bizarre round creature without a head. Later, the Lady told him it was an icon of humanity: directionless, senseless, without a head or tail, in dire need of protection and guidance.

The Lady warned him that there were forces at work to cast the phenomena in a negative light and that if this view won out, humanity would be set on a path to ruin. Chris's work was to prevent this dangerous deception from taking root. She did not explain why, but that he was chosen to tell humanity of the phenomena's benevolence.

"A new knowledge must arrive. Mankind must awaken to it." The Lady of Light's final words were, "This is your burden. You must bear it."

The orbs continued to visit Chris, but the Lady didn't reappear until Easter 2013. Chris was transported by an Orb to a desert area that reminded him of Southern Utah. He landed in a canyon carved deep into the land. The orb bubble popped open revealing three beings like the first time he encountered the Lady of Light with their bodies glowing ivory-yellow like the moon.

Finally, the Lady was there in Light as the canyon gleamed around her bluish-white aura. Her dress was a brilliant white as she sat on a massive stone-carved throne in a recess in the canyon wall. When Chris and the beings approached the front of the throne, the beings gave her a slight bow and turned to walk away, leaving him alone. She stood up from the massive stone throne and hovered over the carved-out canyon floor, never touching the ground. Just forty feet away and twenty feet above him she spoke a parable that took a long time for Chris to decipher.

When the red star of Regulus aligns just before dawn in the gaze of the Sphinx, a new knowledge shall come into the world.

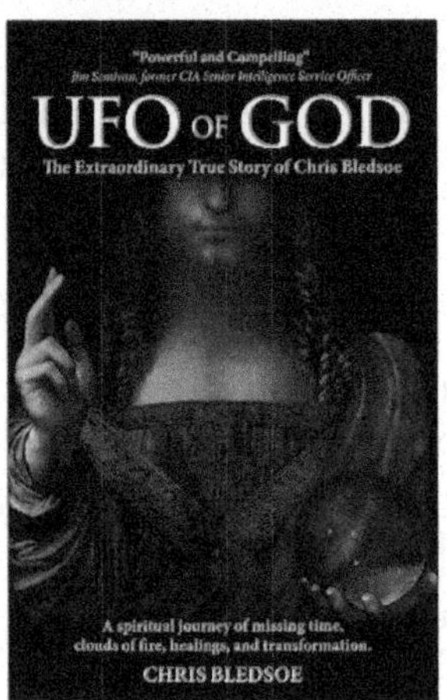

Later Chris was told by an astrologer that Regulus, the brightest star in the constellation Leo, will align with the Sphinx in 2026 close to Easter. The ancient Egyptians saw it in 2372 BCE. According to another astrologer, the Egyptians would have seen Regulus align at midnight in the midheaven on a particular night when it aligned perfectly. This alignment happens once every 25,722 years.

Chris believes The Lady was telling us something wonderful will happen near Easter in the year 2026 that will change humanity from the old ways to a new age.

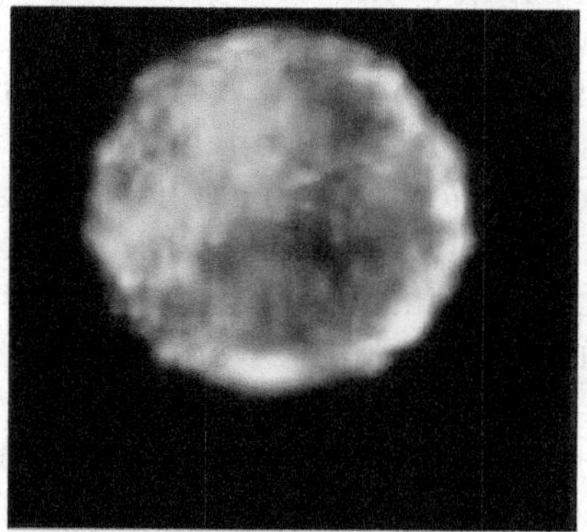

Bledsoe has captured over 2,000 videos of orbs flying over his home in the last two years. Pictured is an up-close image of an orb taken in 2012. It was hovering three feet off the ground when he snapped it 15 feet away

Chris was warned about COVID-19 in 2019 by a tall, majestic figure with broad shoulders. A Jesus figure perhaps, but Chris didn't say in the book. He was told by the being, "We will allow you to film us more and share with witnesses. Share the truth. Difficult times ahead."

Chris sensed the warning meant famine, plague, and unrest would befall humanity soon. Was the entity's warning about Armageddon? Without knowing for sure, Chris didn't want to alarm people if he misinterpreted the message.

I believe Chris is an honest man, telling the truth about his bizarre encounters with otherworldly beings, but was it real or holographic? I have many questions: why was Chris healed of Crohn's Disease, and from the pain of rheumatoid arthritis and other health issues? Why is he required to suffer as the Lady seemed to indicate? I find this disheartening if these entities claim to have our best interest but want us to suffer for it.

What if what Chris witnessed was mind-control used by the CIA from 1953 through the late 1970s, or perhaps a hallucinogenic drug? If the orbs and the Lady of Light are extraterrestrials, they might be colluding with the U.S. secret military and Chris is an experiment to further their Project Blue Beam.

Do you remember Project Blue Beam from the 1990s, a conspiracy theory that a military/government project existed whose purpose was to create an artificial Second Coming? As per the alleged theory, the New World Order's purpose is to abolish all Christian and traditional religions to replace them with a one-world religion and to abolish the family unit today and replace them with individuals all working for the glory of the new One World Government.

Already Christian religion is vanishing as we move closer to a New World Order of Communism.

Much about Chris's story reminds me of the three children of Fatima, Portugal who witnessed a similar Marian entity with orbs or inside of orbs while tending sheep in the town of Fatima on May 13, 1917, at solar noon on the 13th day for five more months through October 13, 1917, when the Lady produced miracles as promised. She appeared in an orb-like Chris's Lady of Light, and she healed many in Fatima. On October 13, 1917, she made the sun spin wildly and appear to fall toward Earth to the horror of thousands gathered that day.

It had rained hard that day and the people were soaked, standing in mud, waiting for the miracle. At solar noon, the rain ceased, and the clouds were pulled apart, revealing what one reliable witness claimed was a disc with a sharp rim and clear edge, luminous and lucent. It was smokey silver in color. The sun does not have a silver color not that anyone has ever observed. The odd thing was that not one astronomer noticed anything usual with the sun on October 13, 1917. Only those gathered within a five-mile radius witnessed the miracle of the sun. What the people described wasn't the sun, but possibly a huge UFO Mother Ship.

The Lady told the children that the two youngest, Francisco, nine, and Jacinta, six, would suffer greatly and die soon, but Lucia dos Santos, nine, would live a long life. The two youngest, Francisco and Jacinta, died from the Spanish Flu raging worldwide at that time. Lucia dos Santos became a cloistered nun and joined the Carmelite order and died on February 13, 2005, in Coimbra, Portugal.

What were the odds of Lucia dying on the 13th day of February, the day of the month the Lady always appeared?

Some say Chris is dealing with demonic forces. They aren't demonic, but they might not be benevolent. Perhaps they use life-like holographic images to deceive us and make us believe they are religious figures seen through the ages. Why was Chris taken to Utah or a desert canyon somewhere in the world, and why not to another planet or space? Why the theatrics?

More questions: why didn't Chris Bledsoe use the beautiful painting of The Lady of Light instead of Leonardo da Vinci's painting *Salvator Mundi* of Jesus on the cover of his book, *UFO of God*? There isn't any mention of Jesus in his book. The Lady of Light appeared to be more benevolent than the dark painting *Salvator Mundi* on his cover. It was a peculiar pick by Chris.

Certain extraterrestrials or whatever they are like to deceive humans and use mind control. Thousands of people claim they have been abducted and told the world is going to end and they are chosen for a special mission, but the mission is never revealed and the world never ends. Many abductees have claimed the aliens controlled their thoughts and bodies. Often abductees feel violated, not only by the experiments conducted on them but also by tampering with their thoughts.

On September 20, 2023, Earth Mysteries Investigator Linda Moulton Howe said on her Earthfiles YouTube channel that a whistleblower knows the JSOC (Joint Special Operations Command) and the Zodiac Special Forces are interacting with "advanced biological AI beings" on Earth at or near Fort Liberty that just happens to be located 11.4 miles north of Fayetteville, North Carolina where Chris Bledsoe resides. Coincidence? Maybe not!

Chris wrote in his book that NASA conducted experiments on his brain to undercover how he communicates with the orb intelligences. Are Chris's entities involved with JSOC and Zodiac Special Forces in northwestern North Carolina not far from Chris's home?

The Map on the next page shows how close Chris lives to Fort Liberty and Pope Field.

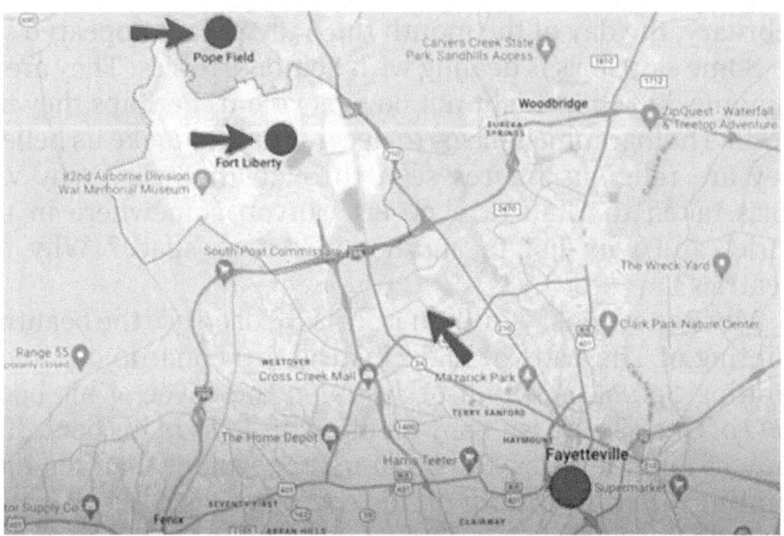

Map of Fort Liberty and Pope Field in North Carolina

Could these special forces be linked to Chris's encounters, and was he programmed during his first encounters in 2007 while on a camping trip when he went missing for over four hours? There is much more going on with Chris's experiences with the orbs and the Lady of Light that might involve the U.S. military. I do not believe that the entities that Bledsoe came in contact with (and is still in contact with) are of Source, the Creator, God, or the fundamental force of creation. It appears to me that whatever these entities are, they are putting a lot of effort into convincing humans they are sent by God when it is far more likely that they are simply creatures from another place or dimension who want human beings to worship them as God for unknown reasons—such as control of the planet? There are many species and beings in our Cosmos, but they are not gods or spiritual just because they have advanced sciences and technology.

Unfortunately, I believe that ultimately Chris Bledsoe is one of the thousands of victims of shadow forces. What Bledsoe and others take from his experiences appears naïve and dangerous.

During my interview on Stargate Radio with Chris on September 7, 2023, Chris discussed how great NASA is and his work with them, and I remarked that our Government/NASA is not as magnanimous as he believes. There are too many horrendous experiments conducted by the U.S. military and Government on people oblivious to their evil experiments like MK Ultra Mind Control from 1942 to 1944, and how the U.S. Chemical Warfare Service conducted experiments that exposed thousands of U.S. military personnel to mustard gas, to test the effectiveness of gas masks and protective clothing. In Vietnam. The experiments involved at least 254 chemical substances, but focused mainly on mid-spectrum incapacitants, such as LSD, THC derivatives, benzodiazepines, and BZ.

NASA has kept the truth for us about what giant structures on the Moon and Mars, and what the astronauts have seen. How can we believe anything they tell us?

The military shot accident victims up with plutonium, tested nerve gas on sailors, and tried LSD hallucinogenic on soldiers. The military continues to push the envelope in seeking new warfare techniques based on cutting-edge science and technology.

Why would my remark upset Bledsoe? Either he is naïve or he has been mind-controlled into believing he was taken to a remote location in southern Utah and introduced to a Marian-looking woman who sat on a throne as ETs bowed to her. What kind of experiments did they conduct on him?

I believe that Bledsoe is a good, honest man who has been used by governmental types steeped in secrecy for control and other experiments. I've read many true stories by abductees that tell of horrendous experiments on them, not just ordinary people but military too. It's time our politicians uncover the truth about UAPs and beings that reside deep underground and in our oceans that our military has known about for decades and continued to work with them.

NASA recently released a report stating that they found no evidence that UFOs are extraterrestrial. Do they mean that UFOs are controlled by earthly beings? Why in the world would NASA bother experimenting on Chris's brain if he's not in contact with aliens or otherworldly beings?

A curious observation made by Chris Bledsoe was the insignia that aliens wore on their suits was similar to President Trump's Space Force emblem. Are Chris's beings time travelers or just deceptive aliens?

The Space Force symbol is on a dark blue disc, between two constellations in white, a light blue globe grid-lined in silver surmounted by a silver delta both encircled diagonally by a white orbit ring, all beneath a white Northern star in the upper left portion of the disc and above the Roman numerals "MMXIX" (year 2019) arching in white.

Betty Andreasson Luca's Encounters

Betty Andreasson Luca, (1937-2022) became well-known from Raymond Fowler's books, *The Andreasson Affair* and *The Watchers I and II* about Betty and her husband Bob Luca's extraterrestrial abductions through the years. Both Betty and Bob felt their experiences were religious in nature and Betty believed the gray beings were angels. Not only did Betty have visitations with the grays, but with the Elders, beings that looked human but identical as if cloned. They wore long robes and conducted spiritual rituals during her abductions.

Andreasson's story began on the evening of January 25, 1967, in south Ashburnham, Massachusetts. The lights went out in her home, and her seven children and her parents, who were visiting, gathered in the kitchen. Her father looked out the back window, attracted by a pink light that was shining, and he saw several little creatures that he thought of as

Halloween-like entities. He made a passing note of them but did not do anything. The next morning, all appeared to be back to normal, except Andreasson had a strange feeling that something out of the ordinary had happened. Over the next few weeks, she had flashbacks of humanoid creatures and an otherworldly environment, but it was not until 1977 when she underwent some hypnosis sessions that the entire story surfaced.

Betty Andreasson Luca was told she was chosen (sound familiar?)

ETs are visiting Earth and there are many species with different agendas. Some view us as children in need of help, others want to experiment on us and genetically alter us as slaves, and others are observing us and probably think we are gullible beings, easily manipulated, and on the verge of destroying ourselves from our ignorance and greed.

More and more ET and UFO whistleblowers will step forward in 2024 and uncover more of the government's secrets and their connection to otherworldly beings and how we are conned by them. There will be some startling revelations forthcoming in the next three years. The reason I refer to them as otherworldly beings is because some of them have lived on Earth for eons.

Humanity is going to discover in a very harsh way that life on Earth isn't all sunshine, lollipops, rainbows, and Jesus!

The Fatima Warnings and Blood Red Auroras

In 1927, Jesus reportedly spoke to Lucia, a Carmelite Nun, and the eldest living child of the Fatima Visions that began in May of 1917 thru October 1917. Jesus instructed her to divulge part of the secret given in July 1917, including what the Lady of Fatima had told her regarding five scourges that were to transpire. He said, "When you shall see the night illuminated by an unknown light, know that it is a great sign that God is giving you that He is going to punish the world for its crimes by means of war..."

That sign, as prophesied, came on the night of January 25, 1938, when all of Europe and part of North America was lighted by an extraordinary, brilliant display of the aurora borealis. World War I was the first scourge, and the second was the militant rise of communism and World War II. Lucia said that if the world ignores the Lady's requests, every nation, without exception, will come under Communist domination. Communism is encompassing the world including America.

From September 23 to September 26, 2023, brilliant red auroras appeared over Europe like they did in 1938. Are we being warned of a great conflagration? My answer is a resounding YES! "These were some of the reddest auroras I've ever seen," says photographer Chris Walker of the Mull of Galloway, Scotland.

Red Auroras are rare. What makes red auroras rare? Partly it's because we have trouble seeing them, so they go unreported by skywatchers. Mainly, though, it's because they are the most delicate auroras. Red auroras come from atomic oxygen near the top of Earth's atmosphere. Oxygen atoms excited by solar wind, or a CME spit out their red photons very slowly. The radiative lifetime of the transition is 110 seconds—in eternity in the quantum realm. The atoms must remain undisturbed for that long to produce their eerie red light.

Pope John Paul II directed the Holy See's secretary of state to reveal the third secret in 2000; it spoke of a "bishop in white" who was shot by a group of soldiers who fired bullets and arrows at him. Many people linked this to the assassination attempt against Saint John Paul II in St. Peter's Square on May 13, 1981. The third secret was revealed to the children at the Cova on July 13, 1917. It was to be kept in the greatest confidence. When Sister Lúcia was with the Dorothean Sisters in Tuy, Spain, she fell ill in mid-1943. Because it was feared that she could die before the third secret was revealed, the Bishop of Leiria requested that she write down the remainder of the secret (or third secret) told to the children in 1917. Obediently, and amid her painful sickness, Sister Lúcia wrote it down on a single sheet of paper. She placed it in an envelope and sealed it.

"After the two parts which I have already explained, at the left of Our Lady and a little above, we saw an angel with a flaming sword in his left hand; flashing, it gave out flames that looked as though they would set the world on fire, but they died out in contact with the splendor that Our Lady radiated toward him from her right hand: pointing to the earth with his right hand, the angel cried out in a loud voice: '*Penance, Penance, Penance!*'

And we saw in an immense light that is God: 'something similar to how people appear in a mirror when they pass in front of it' a bishop dressed in white 'We had the impression that it was the Holy Father.' "Other bishops, priests, men and women religious going up a steep mountain, at the top of which there was a big cross of rough-hewn trunks as of a cork tree with the bark; before reaching there the Holy Father passed through a big city half in ruins and half trembling with halting step, afflicted with pain and sorrow, he prayed for the souls of the corpses he met on his way; having reached the top of the mountain, on his knees at the foot of the big cross he was killed by a group of soldiers who fired bullets and arrows at him, and in the same way there died one after another the other bishops, priests, men and women religious, and various lay people of different ranks and positions. Beneath the two arms of the cross, there were two angels each with a crystal aspersorium in his hand, in which they gathered up the blood of the martyrs and with it sprinkled the souls that were making their way to God. "

The scenes that Sister Lúcia recalled are intense and wildly descriptive. We can only imagine what the three young visionaries experienced and thought upon receiving the great prophetic secrets of Fatima that day. The words and visions given by God and the Blessed Mother are meant for all of us.

Sister Lúcia's Interpretation of the Third Secret

Almost 40 years later, in a May 1982 letter to Pope John Paul II, Sister Lúcia gave an interpretation of the third secret. She wrote: "The third part of the secret refers to Our Lady's words: 'If not, [Russia] will spread her errors throughout the world, causing wars and persecutions of the Church. The good will be martyred; the Holy Father will have much to suffer; various nations will be annihilated.' The third part of the secret is a symbolic revelation, referring to this part of the message, conditioned by whether we accept or not what the message itself asks of us: 'If my requests are heeded, Russia will be converted, and there will be peace; if not, she will spread her errors throughout the world.'

Pope John XXIII decided not to reveal the secret and returned the envelope to the Holy Office. Almost six years later, on March 27, 1965, Pope Paul VI read the contents and decided not to publish it. The envelope was then returned to the Archives of the Holy Office. Not long after he was seriously wounded in a burst of gunfire in St. Peter's Square, Pope John Paul II requested the envelope containing the third part of the secret.

The pontiff had written a message to be read to pilgrims in Fatima to commemorate the anniversary of the apparitions. Astonishingly, this message was being read aloud on May 13, 1981, at the moment Mehmet Ali Agca fired shots at the Pope, who was standing in an open car moving slowly into St. Peter's Square, which was filled with more than 10,000 people.

Pope John Paul II was shot four times and suffered severe blood loss. He was near death when he arrived at Gemelli Hospital. The pope was very moved upon reading the contents of the envelope as the reality of the secret sunk deeper into his heart. He immediately thought of consecrating the world to the Immaculate Heart of Mary.

He believed that on May 13, 1981, which was the 64th anniversary of the first apparition in Fatima, the Blessed Mother guided the bullets that shot him to protect him from death. The third secret of Fatima was so much about him, the "bishop dressed in white." Pope John Paul II recognized himself as the pope (or bishop) who, in the third part of the secret, was killed. However, Pope John Paul II was not killed but was miraculously saved by the Blessed Mother.

Some would later say that Pope John Paul II couldn't possibly be the "bishop in white" in the vision because he did not die. To that, Pope John Paul II answered that he should have died, but the Blessed Mother brought him back from the brink of death. He even went so far as to say that the Blessed Mother gave him back his life.

The third secret of Our Lady of Fatima was made public on May 13, 2000, at the beatification Mass of Francisco and Jacinta Marto. The Mass was held in the Cova da Iria, where Our Lady told the young shepherds the three secrets.

As soon as the third secret was revealed, controversies spread like wildfire. Many questioned whether the Vatican was holding back the full secret. Was the Church revealing the authentic text? Where were the words about an impending great apostasy, a warning of a nuclear holocaust, or about Satan entering the Church? People wanted to believe that the third secret was about impending disasters.

As Cardinal Ratzinger predicted, many were disappointed once the secret was revealed, and for some, disappointment led to suspicion. Many conspiracy theories surfaced. That much of the visions and warnings were redacted by the Church. Did the messages given to Lucia about World War III scorching the Earth, include how cities will fall into ruin by megathrust earthquakes, famine, and plagues?

In my book, *Mystic Revelations of Thirteen*, I suggested that Pope Francis is the anti-pope because of his use of the number 13, an Illuminati number. On March 13, 2013, Cardinal Jorge Mario Bergoglio of Argentina was elected the new pope after Pope Benedict XVI suddenly stepped down on February 28, 2013. Oddly, Bergoglio, born December 17, 1936, was 76 years old when he was chosen pope, a number that totals 13. He decided on the papal name of Pope Francis I in honor of Saint Francis of Assisi, the 13th-century friar and preacher known for his humility toward nature, animals, and the poor.

Is Pope Francis the humble man he portrays? On March 13th, Francis celebrated his tenth anniversary as Pope. The 13th day was important for the Fatima Marian apparition to visit the children in 1917. Fatima was a test by otherworldly beings who have been controlling humanity for eons with holographic inserts of religious figures.

Pope Francis promised to investigate pedophile stories in the Vatican and around the world when he became pope. Not much has been done since he was selected as pope. In 2019, Pope Francis closed a summit on pedophilia by saying that "no explanation suffices" for cases of child sexual abuse within the Catholic Church. You can see his true nature and how little he cares about sexually abused children—he is an anti-pope.

The Vatican and the Catholic Church have a long history of sexual abuse.

Advanced ET Holographic Technology

Humans can change faces, and voices and create any scenario on the internet through AI technology. What is real and what is fake? It's impossible to tell anymore.

Because we live in a frequency-controlled society, the ability of humans to create technologies could be greater. In a less controlled society that has greater outreach or travel capabilities through space and greater interchange between systems, technological advances are quite astounding. It's not that humanity doesn't have great scientists, but most of these inventions were stolen and kept by the Elite. That's what happened to Nikola Tesla's inventions which were far ahead of his time. He believed that one day we would possess the free energy that surrounds Earth—and pollution-free energy.

Many of the amazing things outside this planet have been covered up. A whole new way of influencing and controlling thought was introduced to the planet by the film industry. Now we are learning about holographic technology, but those in space have used this technology for eons. They make holographic inserts—dramas that look real. They are inserted through portals into our reality. Since these space beings have been around for millions of years, humanity's frequencies have been controlled because it is quite easy to fool human beings.

Holographic images have substance and it's nearly impossible to tell if they are real or not. 3-D inserts are meant to be viewed in the sky and to influence large groups of people at once. Think of the Phoenix, Arizona mass UFO sighting on March 13, 1997. Again, the use of the date 13. It was probably a holographic insert. Many but not all UFO sightings are holographic inserts. There have been holographic inserts of one particular religious figure throughout history, designed in many fashions, and projected simultaneously in many different cultures by Other Worldly beings. That is why some of Earth's religious stories are almost identical from one corner of the world to another when there was no physical contact.

Tibet and the Middle East are both dimensional doorways, entryways onto the planet for certain energies. The Middle East is a hot spot for violence and war and that's because it is a portal where many dimensions meet and where entities from other dimensions can come onto the planet. In the last forty or fifty years, many civilizations have surfaced, and many religious dramas have started in the Middle East. Because of the vortex, holographic inserts are easier to produce in that area, just like movies are easier to produce by Hollywood studios.

Many human dramas were holograph inserts to control humans. Since the Middle East is in the midst of a crisis, like other countries of the world, it is a prime candidate for holographic inserts and also prime for a belief system to be altered in our chaotic world. Currently, it is happening in the Mideast war between Palestine and Israel, and it's going to grow into a catastrophic event for many innocent people living there.

An investigation by The New York Times found that many of the troops sent to bombard the Islamic State in 2016 and 2017 returned to the United States plagued by nightmares, panic attacks, depression, and, in a few cases, hallucinations. Once-reliable Marines turned unpredictable and strange. Some are now homeless. A striking number eventually died by suicide or tried to. They are seeing ghosts. Interviews with more than 40 gun-crew veterans and their families in 16 states found that the military repeatedly struggled to determine what was wrong after the troops returned from Syria and Iraq. Was this another secret military experiment on unknowing soldiers?

Be aware of how these dramas make you feel—anger, hate, upset, and how that vibrational energy encompasses the planet.

The three children of Fatima, Portugal experienced a Marian apparition in 1917 on six different occasions, always on the thirteenth of the month and always at solar noon from May to October. The projections were like a movie, but one where humans could interact with the image. You can walk into a holographic image, participate in it, and swear they are real. However, inserts are orchestrated events designed to influence and control the minds of humans. It's all about control!

There are advanced beings so clever they create a reality to hoodwink humans. Holographic inserts are beams of light projected onto this planet through portals. Incredible energy is required due to the process involved in merging dimensions. Technology does not exist in the third dimension, but it exists in other dimensions, and they need dimensional fusions. Why? Each dimension has a different vibratory rate at which the molecules move. These holographic inserts need places where the dimensions are already merged because they need to play through the other dimensions to enter here.

These inserts have been used on Earth to manipulate and control consciousness and to change the story of information to one of disinformation. Those who utilize this technology are not always bringing in light or information. The Lizzies have perfected this technology. They use it to shapeshift their appearance, so humans aren't frightened of their reptilian image. Much of the UFO (Unidentified Flying Objects) and UAP (Unidentified Aerial Phenomena) are holographic images or inserts that appear and disappear at lightning speed.

The portals are also used to travel great distances in a very short time or even travel in time. Holographic inserts are creations of events manufactured and inserted into our reality to look as if they are part of sequential action. They are used to control the minds of the observers, and it's very difficult to tell they are inserts. To an intuitive or sensitive person, they would sense something amiss. Some of the events will be real while others will be inserts designed to move the consciousness of humanity toward the "One World Order."

In the years ahead, we will have plenty of practice viewing holographic inserts around the planet. Humans must learn how to read deceive energies. We must learn to trust our instincts and all our senses.

Scientists have discovered that when you look at something, that moment is already in the past. You think you are perceiving reality with your senses when your brain has limited your perceptions of reality. When you get goosebumps on your arms, the hair on your arms stands on end, or when you get a strange feeling in your gut, or your intuition tells you something is amiss, always trust that feeling. Holographic inserts don't feel right!

If you are a dowser, you can detect these energy fields. Dowsing roads move differently in holographic inserts because their energy fields are diverse and vibrate at an incredible rate.

Portals are also time machines. To traverse certain belts of consciousness you must find the proper portal to come back onto the planet in the precise period or corridor of time that you are looking for. This is how systems are kept locked and intact, and how they are prevented from being raided and taken over. There are portals/stargates located in South America, North America—Skinwalker Ranch, off the coast of So. California, Mt. Shasta in Northern California, Crater Lake, Oregon, Lake Baikal, Russia, Northern and Southern Colorado, Arizona, the Bermuda Triangle, Japan's Triangle, and the Triangle in Alaska, and also Asia, China, England and most of the planet. Of course, the largest portal is located in the Middle East.

Many holographic inserts or dramas have been inserted through that particular portal to create chaos and hate in the minds and beliefs of the population. Beware of how the news media and governments want to affect your feeling centers when dramas happen in the Middle East. Because of the vortex, holographic inserts are easier to produce in that area. A religious figure or the arrival of extraterrestrials could take place there and it will all be a mirage created by 3-D holographic technology.

Planets also have doors through which you can enter portals composed of corridors of time. The Tibetans, until 1950, maintained an energy doorway. Over hundreds of years, they have acted as guardians and emissaries for those who ventured through the portals. According to the same source, Tibetans have been working with extraterrestrials for eons.

In the coming years, you will find your beliefs shattered. You will feel like a child learning Santa Claus isn't real and that your parents deceived you for years.

Scientists have speculated for years that wormholes exist throughout the Universe, a hypothetical structure connecting disparate points in spacetime, and are based on a special solution of the Einstein field equations. A wormhole can be visualized as a tunnel with two ends at separate points in spacetime. Extraterrestrial and dimensional beings have perfected this technology.

Proof Portals Exist at Skinwalker Ranch

During Season 4 of *The Secret of Skinwalker Ranch*, Dr. Travis Taylor and his team believed they found evidence of a portal in what they call the Triangle area on the Ranch located in northeastern Utah. In Season 4, Episode 13, the Skinwalker Team witnessed a large rocket vanish into the Triangle Area of the Ranch at 1:52 am at 10,000 feet, traveling at 800 mph. It broke the sound barrier. Something invisible exists about the triangle, and the team wants to know what it is.

Dr. Travis Taylor, a scientist and engineer, theorizes a transversable wormhole exists above the Triangle where the rocket vanished, and where orbs vanish into the Mesa. The explanation for a transversable wormhole is that if a particle can enter through one side of the wormhole and it can exit through the other, then the wormhole is traversable. Thermal images after the rocket vanished an orb materialized and then the orb split into and then turned into five spheres. UAPs have been seen sliding in and out of the rock Mesa as if it were Jello. Indigenous tribes in the Utah region, Navajo and Utes, have legends of portals and stargates where orbs appear and vanish in an instant.

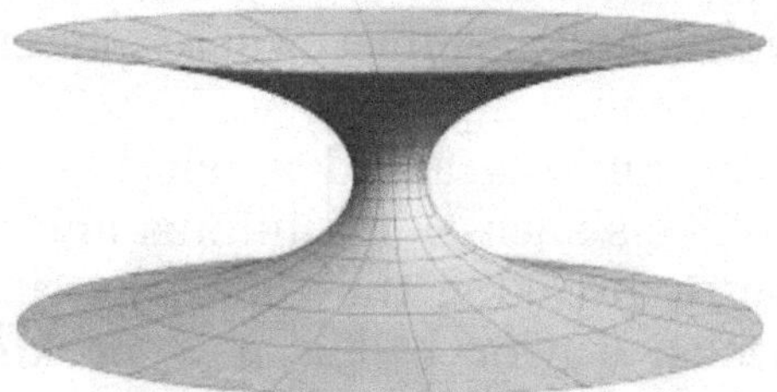

Transversable Wormhole

Thousands of people have witnessed ETs walk through solid objects and into mountains and Mesas. They can manipulate time and space.

Skinwalker Ranch's owner Branden Fugal and the Skinwalker team say that The Secret of Skinwalker Ranch, Season 5 will "break our reality and change world history."

Better stay tuned!

UAP/orb captured over the Skinwalker Ranch Mesa on a 24/7 live stream camcorder.

During another chips and salsa informal chat on October 5, 2023, Brandon and his team met to answer questions for Skinwalker Ranch members. Brandon said Robert Bigelow, the previous owner of Skinwalker Ranch, would never step foot on the Ranch again after seeing the paranormal things there and the hitchhiker effect where poltergeist activity happened in his home.

Dr. Travis Taylor was asked about how UAPs can go through solid objects such as mountains and water without making a wake or breaking the sound barrier traveling at impossible speeds. Taylor called it a pocket reality and mentioned supercavitation. Supercavitation is the use of a cavitation bubble to reduce skin friction drag on a submerged object and enable high speeds or UFOs have an electromagnetic field around them. What if they can shapeshift from a material object into a non-material object with advanced technology? Not only can UFOs go through solid objects, but so can extraterrestrial beings that can walk through walls.

Most often UFOs have a blue aura around them which indicates high voltage. If UFOs were entirely in this dimension, the laws of centrifugal force would be entirely valid for them. Since it is obvious that the effects of centrifugal force have no bearings on their space, and they are moving in time and space.

As Brandon Fugal said, “humanity is not alone in the Universe.” It’s ridiculous to think we are the only ones on this little planet in the entire Universe.

Chaco Canyon’s Portal

Most of you probably can’t comprehend dimensional portals on Earth and throughout our universe. They exist, and people have seen them. They've been here for eons, passed down in legends by indigenous peoples.

Chaco Canyon is located 72 miles south of Farmington, New Mexico, and is the location of monumental structures built by a mysterious people called the Anasazi (or Puebloan people). They built their structures in a hostile environment

1,100 to 1,200 years ago. They left behind rock drawings and petroglyphs of monsters, spirals, dragons, and giants with six toes. The Anasazi were well-versed in mathematics and astronomy.

Chaco Canyon, New Mexico

The Navajo people have legends of the Anasazi people who fought off red-headed giants as tall as 40 feet high who were cannibals. Their stories include a reptilian race called "The Deceivers," and a great flood. The Native Americans in New Mexico believe the spiral petroglyphs tell the story of portals or stargates in the area where bizarre beings travel to and fro from their place of origin in the cosmos.

Dr. David Morehouse, Ed Dames, and Mel Reily decided to investigate Chaco Canyon in the early 1980s and find out if there was any truth to a portal above the Mesa. What they discovered there was beyond their wildest imagination.

Dr. David Morehouse served in staff and command positions ranging from Airborne rifle company commander to commander of an elite Airborne Ranger Company. He was Aide de Camp to two generals, the Battalion Executive Officer of the 680-man 2nd Battalion, 505th Parachute Infantry Regiment, as well as the Chief of Training for the 13,500-soldier 82nd Airborne Division. From 1987 to 1991, David Morehouse was assigned to several highly classified special access programs in the US Army's Intelligence Security

Command and the Defense Intelligence Agency's Directorate of Science and Technology as a top-secret Psychic Spy or Remote Viewer. He holds a Master of Military Art and Science Degree, a master's degree in administration, and a Doctorate in Education. He resigned his commission in 1995 after his decision to write *Psychic Warrior* resulted in the filing of unfounded charges against him, which ultimately were dismissed as baseless by an Army discharge review board.

From 1987 to 1991, Morehouse was assigned to several highly classified special access programs in the US Army's Intelligence Security Command and the Defense Intelligence Agency's Directorate of Science and Technology as a top-secret Psychic Spy or Remote Viewer.

Retired Major Ed Dames was a decorated military intelligence officer, an original member of the U.S. Army prototype remote viewing training program, and a former training and operations officer for the Defense Intelligence Agency's psychic intelligence collection unit.

In the 1980s, Dr. David Morehouse, Ed Dames, and Mel Reily decided to investigate and substantiate the existence of a portal in the southwestern United States near the Abiquiú area, located 53 miles north of Santa Fe. New Mexico. Ed targeted an area in New Mexico where subterranean extraterrestrials supposedly exist.

Eventually, the three men were guided to another area by two Native Americans who told them there was another place to go. They said it was a special place and to expect things to happen at night. At twilight, the men noticed a bright light moving vertically above the horizon and vanished as if it went into the ground. They saw bursts of light and brief objects going from one dimension to another dimension.

Later they went to another area where they were permitted by a Park Ranger to stay in a certain area. Laying on their backs, the three men witnessed the sky become what could only be described as circular translucent water or cellophane as it distorted the night's starlight. They theorized it was a dimensional stargate where space folds in on itself. It was not an atmospheric phenomenon, Dr. Morehouse said. It remained for several minutes, and then collapsed and vanished. It opened three more times in two and half hours, remaining stationary in the sky for fifteen minutes and then closing. Morehouse theorized it remains open for a certain time and then closes if nothing is coming or going through it.

They were unable to capture the phenomena at the time, forgetting cameras. Also, cell phones were invented in 1983, but could not take pictures or videos like the ones used today.

Who were the giants that feasted on Native Americans? Legends of the giants exist throughout the world. Dr. Morehouse in an interview said that archaeologists had discovered bones in Chaco Canyon clearly showing humans were cut up as if feasted.

According to reports of Northern Paiute oral history, the Si-Te-Cah, Saiduka, or Sai'i were a legendary tribe of Northern Paiutes who fought a war with red-headed giants and eventually wiped them out or drove away from the area, with the final battle having taken place at what is now known as Lovelock Cave near Lovelock, Nevada, where they burned them alive.

When you understand how portals exist on Earth and that a plethora of aliens and dimensional beings dominate these portals, you will understand what is currently happening worldwide as humans move closer to World War III. Evil beings have orchestrated the current events. The Mideast has been a major portal where entities control humans and ignite wars, and they feed on human fear, hate, and anger.

CHAPTER SEVEN

THE MIDEAST WAR

There is much propaganda and misinformation about the events taking place in the Mideast to make you angry, fearful, and controlled. The Mideast has a prime giant portal that allows many dark entities into our world. Earth is in dire straits at this time, and there is no doubt about it that World War III looms on the horizon as China moves its naval ships into the Mediterranean, and the United States has moved seven Naval carriers into the region. Iran wants to destroy Israel and the United States if we continue to aid Israel's war against Hamas, the terrorist group controlling Gaza and Palestine. A U.S. nuke sub has arrived in the Middle East, the American military has said in an unusual announcement. The move can be seen as a deterrent to regional adversaries as Iran said the U.S. "will be hit hard" if there is no ceasefire in Gaza.

Many of you feel you have experienced this before. You have! You have experienced wars and chaos in other systems and on Atlantis. This is a prison planet controlled by powerful entities. Humanity is an experiment. The creator gods on Earth now are master geneticists and many of these entities are here to create greater havoc and fear. To gain more control of earthlings, they are going back to their prime portal in the Middle East, where their nest is located deep underground.

The Middle East region has ancient tales of the Jinn or Genies, a being that occupies the shadow world, and also transcends time and physical space. While my cousin Marty lived in Dubai and worked in Iran, he heard stories of the evil Jinn from people who had witnessed them. The Jinn are beings that are part human and part reptilian, and they occupy the largest portal in the Mideast, controlling the people there. They feed off human emotions. They are believed to be the reptilians both benevolent and malevolent.

We are being faced with many opportunities to judge many things, people, and events, and label them as bad. Always remember this is a free-will zone and there is a Divine Plan, the last card to be played. People will protest worldwide over war, Israel, Hamas, Hezbollah, Iran, Ukraine, Russia, China, abortion, Black Lives Matter, or just about anything you can think of in 2024. The fever pitch of the world will grow to insane levels. It's as if everyone has lost their minds, and they have in a sense. Young people are the most vulnerable and gullible and have been easily manipulated with their emotions and thoughts in universities and colleges. They are taught to hate Jews and other nationalities. Most young people have never read anything about the Holocaust in World War II by Hitler and his Nazis, where six million Jews were killed in gas chambers, shot, or starved to death. They can't empathize. Some twisted college students want to kill Jews and have expressed that on internet sites. This is not normal behavior; this is a mental illness.

Did you know that the Ottoman Empire ruled most of the Mideast beginning in 1300? The Empire was ruled by Turks, Arabs, Kurds, Greeks, Armenians and other ethnic minorities. The Ottoman region occupied land in Israel, Syria, Iraq, Egypt, North Africa, Palestine, and even Ukraine. There was mostly peace for 400 years but came to an end in 1932.

I don't foresee the Israel and Palestine war ending soon. Both states are hell-bent on destroying each other. Russia, Iran, and China are all poised to step into the conflict and use nuclear warheads. I foresee a huge conflagration taking place in the Middle East in the coming months if not sooner. We don't realize that these situations are set up to get everyone to think or feel a certain way and to vibrate with a certain consciousness.

The United States is already being drawn into this war that will spread like wildfire to many regions with huge loss of life. Innocent lives will pass, and for what? No one will be the winner, and no one will get what they want from the war. As for Ukraine, the war will continue there as well. Billions of U.S. dollars sent to Ukraine, Israel, and now Palestine will not make a difference.

Hurricane winds of War are whipping around the Earth, showing you there are great stirrings, great deceptions, and great lies to control humanity. Wake up, humanity, and realize who the real deceivers are in our world!

CHAPTER EIGHT

THE AWAKENED ONES

If you are reading this book, you are part of the Family of Light and a system buster. Wherever you go, you facilitate the collapse of systems because you carry light. What is light? It's more than what lights your home and streets. When light changes color and shape or when it flashes across the sky, it shifts your consciousness. Light is information.

We have been taught that we crawled out of caves or were sent away from a perfect garden and then slowly evolved over several thousand years, struggling with a violent Earth and then finally inventing the wheel. But that scenario isn't true. We came from the stars.

Earth and humans are not here as a result of a "big bang" event. Everything is planned, and the universe runs because it is planned. You may not conceive of a universal planner and engineer, however, that doesn't mean it doesn't exist. When we were children there were many things we couldn't imagine that existed in our world. There is so much more to us and the Universe than any of us can fathom.

Our challenge at this time is to gain our freedom back, and this does not mean fighting the government and becoming cannon fodder and becoming victims of mind control, or any other forces that trap you in 3-D. There is a much bigger picture. In dealing with life day-to-day, you probably find yourself questioning your sanity, your purpose in life, and what to do from moment to moment, overwhelmed by what is transpiring in the world at this time. So, get ready, and buckle up for some crazy times ahead.

Our world is one of duality where we dwell. The more light you create the more the shadow defines it. Most of us have been too naïve, and willing to play the game, listening to those in authority who deceive us, and doing what we are told rather than thinking for ourselves. People are not encouraged to think. Mass programming is in effect all over the world and you pay a lot of money for this experience.

That's why this type of misuse of energy has caused people to become disconnected little boxes, compartmentalized fragments with a connection to the whole. That's what they wanted, and they have succeeded. You see when anything becomes fragmented and disconnected in this way, it eventually collapses on itself. Only for a short time can a small part remain isolated.

Look at Mother Earth, the plants, animals, and yourselves, and you discover that you cannot reproduce if you remain isolated. You have been fed a series of false beliefs for thousands of thousands of years, causing each person to become compartmentalized in what each person believes, disconnected from real thinking from yourself and other humans.

The ancients were in contact with the Stars as well as Earth, and they understood everything has a consciousness and is alive. There were those from our ancient past that controlled us, and they still exist. Now with the compartmentalization of people, the gears of old Earth laws are grinding our civilization to a screeching halt. This can be seen in part as people lose jobs, and their homes, and have greater credit card debt than they ever had because of inflation. We are losing touch with practical living and common sense.

Humans are moving too fast and have more technology. As things go faster, we need to slow down and take time to listen to nature, the birds, a crackling fire, and other natural sounds. Get outdoors and away from the cities that are crumbling before our eyes.

We need to trust the voice in our heads that the ancient Egyptians called *Ka*. Reach out in times of trouble to your higher consciousness. It is an important key to know yourself and an essential tool for survival in these coming times. As our system collapses, and it will, and familiar comforts disappear very rapidly in the next few years, there will be an equal number of opportunities. A force of psychic spiritual energy will explode, creating many rapid changes on a planetary scale. There are those among you who have received the messages for beings of Light. These changes will herald a new way of thinking and perceiving, where you will link up as one humanity.

But much of what we perceive as evil will take place, a cleansing of Earth, before we become a spiritually evolved species.

Because of unknown plans, great energy surges and geophysical Earth changes are occurring at a rapid rate, and our electronic grids will break down. Then what would you do if you purchased an EV (electronic vehicle) and got stuck without any power for days, or months? Many of you will find yourselves in the situation of here today, gone tomorrow. Will there be electricity? Will there even be food and water? Will you stock up and be ready for the fast-coming events?

Today the New World Order has a chance to be another Roman Empire. The Roman Empire merged with Christianity in the early centuries of this era and modulated the truth of the Family of Light to fit their political agenda. Will those of you who are bringers of the truth today modulate your truth to be one with the New World Order? Will you align with darkness or light?

Thousands and thousands have gone to the Family of Dark, and they work everywhere and in every occupation. The ancient Christians were divided; far from being unified and were diversified in their teachings. Can you see the parallel with the Republicans and Democrats? Those who speak the truth will be persecuted—pro-lifers, Christians, parents fighting against transgenderism pushed on their children in schools, woke teachings, and CRT (Critical Race Theory). We've seen how anyone who tries to stop the Family of Dark is jailed, fired, or censored.

Migrant children are taken across the U.S. border for the sex trade happening worldwide. Child pornography and child slavery, the slavery of men and women, have always been common. These dark things have been part of Earth's history and have never been studied in classrooms. Perhaps we should consider studying the dark in schools devoted to the dark misuse of power through sex.

In some cultures of the world, the dark forces are acknowledged, and offerings are made, tokens left. Even in the practice of exorcising entities attached to humans an offering of food or a piece of sweets is used to pull the entity into the offering. Newspapers, television networks, and social media are all owned and operated by a small handful of powerful dark individuals. True ownership of these enterprises is difficult to track because there are plans within plans and players behind players, and nothing is exactly as it appears. It is time to walk up and realize that you are fed information designed to limit and control you, to have you support and become part of the economy of death.

Their plans began a long time ago when you were asleep but in 2016, Donald Trump threw a monkey wrench into their plans by getting elected President, and now they are worried he will be back in 2024. They are in for another surprise!

Humans turn a blind eye to malevolent things in life and turn their children over to a Big Brother, mind-control World Management Team where one does not think but simply performs at warp speed or is eliminated. It has become clear that perverted sexual practices by our world leaders are happening. Those in the highest positions have been put there because they are qualified by their perversions to hold power over others. People who have tried to reveal these evil people have died under mysterious circumstances. This has been a secret for eons, but today everyone is coming out of the closet in public. We are already seeing transgender people holding high offices and cross-dressing.

Some believed there was more than one God and others believed in one God. Those who believe there was one God are right. The only true God is LOVE. Those who harm children, animals, and adults are devoid of love.

Angry protests will increase from people around the globe, and the energies will intensify to outrageous states—energies that demand change, some through violence. If you think the shocks and scandals are over—just wait and you will see things the likes of which you have never seen before. You will awaken to see that what is happening in your country, is happening everywhere. It's as if everyone drank tainted Kool-Aid. You are now witnessing tyranny worldwide. Remember in the Bible where people were once divided by the Tower of Babel, when the Gods came down and told humans, "These people are unifying and pretty soon they will be greater than we are. Let us confound their tongues and divide them." And suddenly diverse languages were created.

Today, few people are bilingual or trilingual. Today we are isolated and compartmentalized in our little houses, unconnected to our neighbors or the globe, yet we claim to be a global community alive through electronics, as if the longevity of the globe, alive for billions of years, does not register. Remarkable!

If you ask most college students they have no idea about the making of the U.S. Constitution, the Declaration of Independence, or who our first president of the United States was and what war he fought in. And now to divide us further from our roots, millions and millions of illegals storm the United States borders from every country throughout the globe with no education, skills, or use of the English language. They consist of terrorists, drug cartels, murderers, and rapists crossing our border freely thanks to President Biden who open the borders to all in 2020 when he was elected. There are no jobs for these millions of desperate people (not all criminals) who think the Biden administration will care for them with free housing, healthcare, cell phones, iPads, and food for the rest of their lives while U.S. citizens suffer on the streets without a home.

What do you think will happen when these millions and millions discover they were lied to about the Promised Land in America? Rebellion and civil war. They will take what they want and if you think you are safe in your home, think again. No one will be safe from their anger, desperation, and terror. The United States can't support 7 or more million illegal migrants flooding the borders, and eventually, Americans will be lost and ruined by illegal immigrants who speak many languages and refuse to conform to U.S. laws.

Have you noticed it takes at least two months to see a specialist doctor or even your family doctor? Just wait as millions and millions of illegal migrants require free health care and will be inundating our hospitals, doctors, and care facilities. You may need to wait for a year to get in or more. Biden wants to take care of illegals first! Biden is also giving 500,000 illegal Venezuelans social security cards. Who will hire these unskilled people? Will the small businesses of America be forced to hire them? What will happen to all the U.S. children who won't get an education because of these immigrants?

U.S. President Joe Biden has allowed record numbers of migrants to cross into our borders states illegally since he took office in 2021 and is already facing attacks over the issue as he runs for reelection in 2024, as well as his criminal activities with his son Hunter from taking millions of dollars in bribes from foreign countries. Republicans blame Biden for reversing the hardline immigration policies of former President Donald Trump, the frontrunner for the Republican party's nomination.

Have you noticed it takes at least two months to see a specialist doctor or even your family doctor? Just wait as millions and millions of illegal migrants require free health care and will be inundating our hospitals, doctors, and care facilities. You may need to wait for a year to get in or more. Biden wants to take care of illegals first! Biden is also giving 500,000 illegal Venezuelans social security cards. Who will hire these unskilled people? Will the small businesses of America be forced to hire them?

Today, I watched illegal migrants on the streets of New York City covering their faces and wondered what are they afraid of. Are they wanted criminals in their country? The increase of illegals has strained U.S. cities across America and even on the Canadian/U.S. border. The mayor of Eagle Pass, Texas, declared a state of emergency recently due to a "severe undocumented immigrant surge" into the city as several thousand migrants reportedly arrived in recent days, but still Biden and the "do nothing" Congress can't get anything done or agree on anything.

John Titor claimed to be a time traveler and an American Soldier from the year 2036. He began blogging in the year 2000 and discussed his timeline. He said that Republicans and Democrats started a civil war in the United States. If things continue as they have with both parties dividing the nation, that prediction will come true. As a result, the United States would split into five regions based on a variety of factors, including differing military objectives. Then World War III would break out, but he didn't give the details. He specified Washington, D.C., and Jacksonville, Florida as cities that would be hit in the exchange (nuclear perhaps), and said that after the war, Omaha, Nebraska would be the new U.S. Capitol. In one post, he said that the hostilities were led by "border clashes and overpopulation." He also pointed to the contemporary Arb-Israeli conflict not as a cause of the war, but as a milestone that precedes it.

Titor's last blog was in 2021, and then he vanished. Re-read what he predicted and look at the current situation in the United States and the world. Titor did give a caveat that timelines can be altered. What happened in his timeline 2036, may never happen in our timeline. But at the moment, it seems we are on a runaway train headed for Titor's frightening future. God help us!

Are you praying with all your heart that this madness stops? It's a sin against God that millions of humans live under tyranny and dictators, yet they do. Since Biden became President, the United States has allowed 7 to 10 million refugees worldwide and some of them are drug cartels, sex traffickers, criminals from their country, and now we have enough fentanyl coming into the U.S. to kill the entire U.S. population. How can we afford to help the entire world who wants to live and work in America?

The current Federal debt for the United States stands at $33 trillion and growing fast with the Biden Administration giving Ukraine $75 billion with no accountability. In the present timeline, America will become another third-world country with a dictator as President.

The State of Pennsylvania announced on September 19, 2023, that it has implemented automatic voter registration to ease the process of casting an election ballot, joining 23 other states and the District of Columbia. Residents who are eligible to vote and who obtain or renew a driver's license or identification card at Pennsylvania's Department of Motor Vehicles will not be guided through the voter registration process by default.

Can you see what is going to happen here? It's called voter fraud to stop former President Trump from being elected. They will do anything to stop him, including prison on indictment charges.

Biden did not win the 2020 election fairly and those who claim he did are wrong. That's what they want you to believe but there is plenty of evidence of election tampering in 2020. Remember Biden asked the FBI, and social media giants like Twitter and Facebook to censor any information that could harm his presidency, including information on COVID-19, the use of Ivermectin to cure COVID-19, and Biden's son Hunter and his involvement with receiving large amounts of money in the millions from Ukraine's Burisma energy company, and dealings with China for special favors.

If the public had known about the Bidens and their corruption, would he have still been elected despite those who hated Trump? We will never know.

Everyone knows by now that Hunter Biden smoked crack cocaine and hired prostitutes. He was high all the time. But did he quit? Nope! Cocaine was found at the White House on Sunday, July 2, 2023, but none of the security cameras caught the culprit. How odd! Then on July 4, 2023, Joe and Jill Biden stood on the White House balcony waving as Hunter fidgeted on the balcony with his daughter and paced back and forth. Suddenly, he put his daughter down and left the balcony as if needing another fix. People commented on him sweating and extremely nervous, all signs of cocaine use.

As they say, like father, like son!

If you try to search for certain information, Google, YouTube, Facebook, and the rest of the internet companies make sure anything that looks like a conspiracy is called "misinformation." Often articles are removed. This is Marxism to control what information you get online.

Because everyone is so frightened of giving up the same old system in the United States, they are going to be forced to give it up. The system is corrupt and so are the people who run the country, both Democrats and Republicans. I'm not saying all are corrupt. If something does not honor life and does not honor Earth, you can bet it is going to fall, and it is going to fall big time.

Consciousness must change. This is part of the Divine Plan, and this opportunity and setup are not going to be missed. There has been a complete lack of understanding of the nonphysical world that exists all around us, so there will be a reprioritizing of what comes first in life. People will stand up, who had never thought of standing up before when everything is taken from them.

Our modern technology is one of the biggest weapons for frequency control. We have devices for entertainment and convenience, and they are all involved with frequency control. It would be best to get rid of your television sets because they manipulate your consciousness on a day-to-day basis. The technology is so finely tuned that you respond subliminally to disease via the television. The fear frequency was used to spread COVID-19 worldwide, and it worked well. There is an entire generation that is killing themselves by watching television and its poisonous rhetoric. Even spiritual television shows have implanted material controlling your brain. The subliminal keeps you immobilized and holds you in a "survive, arrive, be-on-time agenda, be silent, go-to-work" society. Television also promotes inactivity and a sedentary, obese lifestyle. Wake up, humans! Can't you see that a huge percentage of humans are huge, sickly, and don't care about their image?

If you think that Dr. Anthony Fauci is a nice grandfather type of scientist, think again. The man was deeply involved with gain of function experiments in Wuhan and at a Montana Lab where a low-rated zoo gave the National Institutes of Health where several bats were infected with a coronavirus from the same Chinese Wuhan lab that some Federal Agencies believe is responsible for the SARS-COV-2 outbreak, according to a new investigation and published research. The White Coat Waste Project, which fights taxpayer funding of "wasteful government animal experiments," said on October 30, 2023, it's using the Freedom of Information Act requests to get more details about the taxpayer-funded experiments documented in a 2018 paper in the Journal Viruses.

Former National Institutes of Allergy and Infectious Diseases Director Dr. Anthony Fauci oversaw the NIH's Rocky Mountain Laboratories in Montana when it did the research with bats from Maryland's Catoctin Wildlife Preserve, whose Director of Animal Health Laurie Hahn is a former NIH "lead veterinary technician" for animal research. The facility is still operating and experimenting with COVID-19 on bats, monkeys, and dogs.

Hahn has been frequently identified as the "curator" of the zoo going back to 2017, a role that encompasses "acquiring animals, transferring animals, research, and other duties related to managing the zoo's population of animals," Goodman said. Her involvement is especially likely "in this case where they have a personal history with the recipient," Hahn's former employer NIH.

WCW provided *Just the News* an Agriculture Department inspection report from April that shows the zoo had 241 bats,

41 of the Egyptian fruit bats used in the NIH research. Its blog post notes USDA fined the zoo $12,000 in 2012 for five years of violations including poor treatment of animals and failure to adequately train a zoo worker who was mauled as a result. Charity Navigator, which rates nonprofits based on several metrics, gives the zoo a 56% rating and one out of four stars due to missing "accountability metrics" among other lapses. The zoo did not immediately respond to a query Monday to confirm what role if any Hahn played in the decision to give her former employer the 12 Egyptian fruit bats.

As comedian George Carlin once said, "I have certain rules I live by. My first rule: I don't believe anything the government tells me."

If you look for the mRNA COVID-19 vaccine and how it has harmed millions of people worldwide with horrible side effects, you find all kinds of disclaimers on internet search engines that discredit the truth and call it conspiracy theories. How can it be a conspiracy theory if thousands have died suddenly after receiving the COVID-19 vaccine from blood clots, myocarditis, and strokes? We are to believe everything the Biden Administration tells us.

The Family of Dark hides the truth and lies to confuse us and have greater control over humanity.

Subliminal Programming

The use of subliminal programming was created to upset human consciousness. If you own two or more television sets in your house, you will probably agree this has been a very successful marketing program. No one is immune to the programming on television even if you wear a tin foil hat on your head. Some entities feed off our emotions. All over the world, billions of humans are emitting emotional energy into the atmosphere based on what they are watching on television each day. Constant negative news harms the human body.

If you really want to evolve, do not read biased newspapers, beware of what is on social media and Chinese-owned TikTok, and stay away from television. TikTok knows everything about you, and it will be used against you in the future. Beware!

If you can be media-free for long periods, and you disengage yourself from the frequency of chaos, anxiety, and stress, you will become clear. You will begin to listen to what is going on inside yourself and to live in the world, not necessarily be lost in it. Television isn't bad, it's just how it is being misused. Tune into God instead.

We keep hearing stories of governments using frequency waves like the strange reports from the American Embassy in Cuba where people suddenly experienced a range of symptoms from pain and ringing in the ears to cognitive dysfunction. It was first reported in 2016 by U.S. and Canadian Embassy Staff in Havana, Cuba. Beginning in 2017, more people, including U.S. Intelligence and military personnel and their families, reported having similar symptoms in other places, such as China, New Delhi, India, Europe, and Washington, D.C. Later it was dismissed as radio waves and nothing more, but it was far worse and kept quiet.

Specific megahertz frequencies can be harmful. Many frequencies are specifically designed to jam our frequency and to keep humans at a certain vibratory rate, turning humanity into safe, harmless, inactive, productive cattle.

Do you think of your laptop or computer as harmless? Think again.

Most of what is being taught to our children and those in college is malarky and damaging. We are told that we can't accomplish anything in life without a degree, but that is false thinking. Come up with a method to explore the world and all the ancient knowledge out there without a degree. Schools are indoctrinating children to be distrustful, bigoted, and hate certain ethnic groups. Whites are evil, your parents are evil and Jews are evil, are just a few of the things they are taught. Instead, the young generations should be taught about nature, their intuition, history, math, astronomy, art, and higher sciences. Children should be seated in a circle, so everyone is equal like King Arthur's court where his knights sat equally at the round table. Much of history has been rewritten to control you and your belief in the world.

As I wrote in my 2022/2023 prediction book, *Prophecy Now*, about abortion, humans have taken the soul equation out of the miracle of birth. Women are told that a fetus isn't a living, breathing being with a soul. That soul may have waited many lifetimes, perhaps even thousands of lifetimes to reincarnate in the right body for further lessons of love, compassion, and forgiveness.

There are so many methods of contraception for men and women that abortion shouldn't exist, except in emergencies where the mother and child are in danger. Humans no longer honor life and the Creator that gave all souls life, including non-humans.

The pro-life/abortion issue has been purposely orchestrated in the United States by different factions within the government to create a lack of harmony. It's called Divide and Conquer to own the people. Whenever people oppose people, those in control benefit, even with the issue of abortion.

How do they benefit? They keep women from uniting with each other and men from uniting with each other. They keep people in fear. They convince you by continuously putting these issues before you, and that you have no control over the birthing processes in your body. A woman doesn't need an abortion; they never need to get pregnant in the first place if they don't desire it. How? By the power of the mind over your body. A woman can say to herself, "I am not prepared at this time for a child." The waiting soul hears this command and will not enter the body. Ancient women understood this sacred knowledge of birth control to stop souls from entering their bodies.

Birth control isn't just a woman's responsibility. Men also have a responsibility for a woman's pregnancy. Our current world offers contraceptives to stop pregnancy for men and women. Life is sacred, and killing an infant fully developed up to nine months old will damage the soul of the woman who decides on such a murderous act. Each soul was created by God to evolve spiritually into a physical body and experience lessons of growth.

How can we determine when the soul enters the fetus? There

will come a day when this becomes possible.

Certain people refuse to define a woman, and a certain group of trans women (males at birth) want to destroy real women and women's sports. They will never be real women in this lifetime. It's time for women to come together and push back on all the terrible things taking place across the country in women's sports, the abortion issue, and women in leadership positions. What ever happened to the Women's Liberation movement that began in the 1960s when women wanted to be liberated and empowered? It is time again for women to heal the Earth and to bring themselves into a place of empowerment. Women are the healers, the medicine women of the past, and the keeper of ancient sacred knowledge.

Violence and drugs on the streets of major cities are another means of control. The big cities in the United States—Los Angeles, New York City, Washington, D.C., and so on—are energy vortexes or holes, where energy comes into the North American continent. There has been a huge increase in violence, looting, and lawlessness in these cities because it is known that if unrest can be kept brewing and reported by the news, it can be a likely vehicle for manipulating the entire nation. These things are purposely set into motion on the physical level and assisted on the etheric level because the more fear that is generated, the more those in charge can control us and feed on it.

Psychiatrists claim that the young men looting and committing violent acts never had a father. The lawless youth of America have never been taught that their actions have consequences not only in this life but the life beyond. As more of us become sovereign and in charge of our own frequency, those who do not want the new frequency here will bring an opposite frequency to create chaos, confusion, and polarity. Always, whenever a society is on the verge of a huge leap or change, there are opposing activities. We can change anything we want to change.

Why do you think you chose to be here at this specific time in history? Certainly not to sit on your couches, eat toxic food, and watch programs that diminish your mental capacity. No, you came here to show the Family of Dark that they can't succeed in the presence of the Family of Light. Light always trumps the Dark (no pun intended for Donald Trump). It won't be an easy task, but it's not impossible.

It is time for us to redefine our own identities in a much greater sense. Events are transpiring in the cosmos that you and even man of our political leaders have no idea of. It's time to realize not all otherworldly beings that come to the planet with advanced sciences and technology are spiritually connected. We are going to discover some very disturbing ideas over the next few years. We must be more discerning about what and who is coming from the skies because we are going to be duped and tricked and most of the people on this planet will not understand it. We are easily duped and tricked. Look at your children who live on TikTok and think what they see is real or true. TikTok currently is running an ad on Fox News that 'TikTok sparks Good'. What a mind-control joke!

Can you sense the confusion and anger spreading around the world? Earth has operated on a very low frequency for a very long time and that frequency is based on survival and disempowerment. Feel the fear and uncertainty running through the lives of people as they begin to realize that the way their lives have been defined is now falling apart. Realize that Light is the culprit of this crumbling that each of us, as members of the Family of Light is causing to take place because you and everyone carry the electromagnetic charge onto Planet Earth that broadcasts the new frequency. You helped create this chaos of new consciousness. You create your reality by your thoughts—it's that simple.

Think about Earth and the destruction taking place on the planet. Our biosphere, our backyards, fields, streams, oceans, rivers, creeks, meadows, and creatures are in jeopardy. The places where children used to play and run by streams or spend afternoons under trees, studying clouds in clear blue skies are slowly disappearing. Magic was once alive. People would rather destroy beauty than appreciate it. Most on this planet have become selfish, narcissistic beings who have become numb to emotions. Many dumb their emotions through drugs and alcohol and never grow spiritually.

There is such a darkness on Earth that it's permeable and it's so vast that many of you are frightened to live. That's their agenda. Our bodies are filled today with cancers, stress, and pollution because we have been primed for fear over the years and have drawn negative energies from other realms. These spirits of lower energies feed off our fear. Through meaningless data, commercials, and meaningless living, you have drawn to you those who remove your power. How do we escape their energy removal by loving ourselves and claiming our power? As we move forward and understand the unfolding absurdity of our times and why our civilization is collapsing, honor yourselves as powerful, spiritual beings.

In time, we will have the ability to shift our perceptions and rebuild our civilization based on value and respect for all life—children, women, men, animals, trees, plants, ocean life, and birds. Healing is coming even though at first it will appear as if our world has been rent asunder. There are hard times ahead. Will you run and be a coward, or stand up with your held head high and help others? Only can the shatter bring about rebuilding.

Jesus said two thousand years ago, "As you think, so shall it be. Do unto others as you would have them do unto you."

This is happening again as history repeats itself when the Family of Light goes before the gladiators. Will we unite or splinter and fracture as we have done in the past few years? We are completely divided, and that's what the Family of Dark has been up to. We are surrounded by all kinds of realms assisting us, however, it all depends on us waking up to our power by being brave, and not accepting the untruths erupting from the mouths of those who could care less about you—The Family of Dark.

Because this is a free-will universe, all of the negativity, wars, greed, and fear have been allowed. The *Creator of All that this Is* is dark and light and all things. It's hard to fathom a creator as dark as well as light, but the Creator is learning about self and growing and expanding.

Who is going to bail you out of this mess of a world where tyranny reigns? Where is the rescue team? Guess what—we are it! We are the ones we've been waiting for. We each came to Earth to do a task, and that mission is now. It's time to trust your inner Cosmic Knowing, that if you think something, it is!

Things will become even more topsy-turvy and chaotic if you haven't prepared, it could be too late. You will be washed into the undertow of the tidal wave as it comes, perhaps literally in the next few years. Ask your guides and angels to keep you, your family, and friends safe in all things.

Say this, "It is my intention that I be always safe and successful in all things that I do. It is my intention to honor my mission and help others." Intend that all assistance comes from LIGHT. Entities can be brilliant and learn to transcend human laws, and yet not operate with the frequency of light and love. There are dark entities that want to control humans by deception. Be clear about the assistance you call in.

We dream of a golden age where everything is perfect and in harmony. But we must consider the wounds of darkness that need to be healed, it may be a long time in human years, but Evil can be transformed.

Many different beings are entering our world. Some view us as laboratory mice to be studied. Some view us with the kindest of intentions and watch us flourish and accept our faults. Others see us as children who need parenting as they are here to support us—not punish us. They want us to learn our lessons with kindness and support. They are like parents who find it important to spend time with their children, to communicate directly with them as the ancients did, rather than park them in front of an electric television as many parents do. How can you learn lessons without diversity?

Our world turned upside down in 2001 when the New York City Trade Towers fell by terrorists (or so we were told), and 2,996 souls died. Then another Prime Event orchestrated to divide and conquer us happened in 2020 due to COVID-19. The Family of Dark locked us down and took away a multitude of our freedoms such as the ability to reject an untested vaccine and to speak our minds without rejection. Jobs were lost when people refused to get the untested vaccine, businesses were lost and nearly three million people died from COVID-19. The Family of Dark planned these draconian agendas ever so discreetly years and years ago. And no one was paying attention. We were too wrapped up in our little world and our lives to notice what they were planning covertly. Each year more of our sovereignty has been taken from us and it continues. People like Hillary Clinton and Joe Biden continued to berate Trump supporters. Hillary recently stated in an interview that MAGA (make America Great Again) followers should be de-programmed, and she had suggested last year that Trump followers are "deplorables." President Biden has called MAGA supporters "white supremacists." How ridiculous to call American citizens such horrible things just to get you to support their Left agenda. He's as evil as the others who want to destroy America and the good people of America.

We have never been so divided—friends, family, politicians, leaders, college students against Jews, blacks against whites, and Muslims against Jews are now enemies. If you were aware, you'd understand this dark plan.

In March 1799, Patrick Henry said these famous words during the Revolutionary War in America, "Uniting we stand, by dividing we fall!"

ho really cares to save a world in despair...when I look at the world it fills me with sorrow... What a shame, such a bad way to live...Live life for the Children...You see, let's save the Children of the World." — Save the Children by Marvin Gaye

CHAPTER NINE

SAVE THE CHILDREN OF THE WORLD

While the left-controlled media pronounced the *Sound of Freedom* movie as some kind of QAnon production for daring to tell the truth about international child trafficking, Vox News went one further by declaring that the movie is "as dangerous" as the practice of child trafficking itself. Vox is an American news and opinion website owned by Vox Media. The website was founded in April 2014, by Ezra Klein, Matt Yglesias, and Melissa Bell.

The Vox article published July 14, 2023, parrots every other hit piece in declaring the movie to be a "giant dog whistle for Qanon recruitment", which is a lie! It also states that the "rugged individualism and masculine rogue operatives on display" in the film are "precisely tailored to cater to views of idealized America."

The people who claim it is a dangerous movie, are the ones pushing sex trafficking. Our country is full of evil and sick people who don't care about children. Then it asks "Can such faith-based cultural products even exist at this point, let alone serve their specific malnourished target audience, without also fomenting extremist rhetoric, bigotry, and attacks on progressive ideals?"

The ludicrous piece then claimed that the film "keeps us from scrutinizing hyperbolic, alarmist cries about child trafficking too closely," before labeling it "a form of extremist propaganda" and asserting it is "at least as dark and dangerous as the very thing *Sound of Freedom* wants to combat."

How can anyone rationalize innocence babies and children sacrificed being sacrificed to drug cartels for sex trafficking? These precious souls are being destroyed by pure evil. Children disappear every day by pedophiles, and many are murdered and never found again. Not only have American children vanished, but children all over the world. And now since Biden has opened our borders to the world of criminals, drug cartels, and terrorists, some children are killed for their organs. You can't even imagine what is going on in the underworld of criminals who have no feelings or emotions for children. Children are like cattle, a commodity for them to be sold as slaves and sexually abused.

These evil people think that what they do will not incur any consequences. There is one Creator and if these predators think they will go to some special place after death and be rewarded, they are in for a shock. What kind of world will this generation see–a world of hate, violence, and devastation? We are headed there. Our children are being abused and mind-controlled. They can't be children anymore, and now we have teachers in schools telling them what sex they can be. Graphic sex books given to children should be banned from schools.

A mother was outraged recently at her child's school at Hillsborough County Public School in Tampa, Florida who was giving out copies of the best-selling pornographic book *Blankets* by Craig Thompson that contains graphic illustrations of sex for boys with boys and boys with girls. The Mother read excerpts from the book at a School Board Meeting and when she held up a graphic image from the book, a policeman took it away. Funny how it's okay for kids to read pornographic literature, but not adults.

Churches and leaders worldwide claim they worship God, but for many, their God is Satan, a demon who they believe will control the world one day. The only problem with this one-sided thinking is that the Universe and God won't allow this great imbalance.

Biological men are destroying girl's sport by competing with them as transwomen. Biological men are built differently than women and have greater strength than women. Shouldn't they have their own category of sports? They should not be allowed in women's bathrooms and dressing rooms. Young girls have been raped in school by boys claiming to be trans when they are heterosexual. It's alarming how this is allowed to happen in schools.

My friend Bob Luca and his wife Betty Andreasson Luca had many experiences and encounters with benevolent beings and became renowned by author Raymond Fowler in his book, *The Watchers,* and *The Watchers II*. They told Bob that we are constantly being monitored. Nothing that we do in our lives escapes them. The Universe is a recorder. Your life, your existence on the Earth plane, is all recorded from the time you were born until the time you die; everything is there. This process determines how rapidly you will advance what your next step or phase will be, what teaching you need to receive, and what hardships you must undergo to deepen your understanding. It's all recorded.

When asked if he was saying that on some level life is fair by the hypnotist, Bob replied, "Life is wonderfully fair. Those of us on this plane just don't understand it. When you see a small child who becomes ill and dies, people weep, they cry, and they grieve. They grieve for themselves. The child does not need to be here any longer. The child has already advanced, much as you would skip a grade school. It is not a bad thing. People that are sick or injured...their faith is being tested. The reactions are recorded. This determines whether or not they need more teaching. They need to advance spiritually. Can they go the next step? Is there more they must learn? When the physical body leaves, you do not die. The physical body has died, and that is not the person. Life is stages, like a never-ending school.

"Without those who are detrimental to society, those who are advanced cannot be tested. Evil serves a necessary purpose. Without all evil to overcome, the righteous could not advance and triumph. It's all part of the system, the order of things, just as the planet must rotate about the sun. There must be sorrow. There must be suffering, because without these things, there is no advancement and nothing to overcome."

The hypnotist then asked Bob, "Are you saying that evil is positive?"

Evil on an earthly plane is the negative aspect. Evil on the larger plane is part of the overall plan that gives us all a chance to advance and rise about it. Everyone on the earthly plane can do evil. Those who don't—those who fight evil, those who learn and overcome evil, those who have advanced—have gained tremendously in the next realm. Everything in nature has a plus and a minus, a light and dark, a negative and positive, a good and bad. It must be, for without some content of evil, there can be no good. There can be no growth."

Bob went on to explain, "We do not need evil for good. We need a choice. The Creator gave us choices. We cannot use that choice unless we have two choices to make. Evil or good. It is so simple. It's beautiful. I don't know how to explain it any other way. As we evolve there will be more good due to those who are advancing. But there will be some very distressing times before that happens. There will be much dissension. There will be more conflict. There will come a time when evil will be wiped away. That time is not close at hand.

"When that time comes, our growth will not cease. Rather, we will advance into further planes of existence. Right now, the type of society that you speak of is not possible because people on this plane as a whole are not very advanced spiritually. Technology is advancing but not spirituality."

The sad part of what is happening is that universities like Yale and Cornell are teaching young people Marxism, and how to hate others. Our youth are being introduced to this indoctrination even in K-2 schools (Kindergarten). They learn to celebrate terrorists. Harvard's Chief Chaplain, Greg Epstein is an atheist, raised in a Jewish household. Harvard University was originally founded with a mission to educate clergymen to minister to New England's early Puritan colonists, and now Harvard has a Chaplain who teaches atheism.

What happened to faith and spirituality in America, the foundation for our Constitution? In God We Trust was a political motto that goes back to the Civil War.

Some students are threatening Jewish students by encouraging other Hamas groups to follow Jews from school to their homes and slit their throats. The FBI is currently looking for these evil monsters who have no respect for life. Who are the Generation X parents of these demented kids? How could they teach them such a horrible philosophy of hate and murder?

In Palestine, school children are taught math by using dead Jews as an example. What do you think mind-controlled children, like those in China, will become as adults? They will become radical thinkers who will lack empathy or compassion for life. It will be easy to kill another human being.

What you do to others, you unto GOD. We are all the essence of GOD, the creator of *All that Is*. God is in each of us.

There is Karma for countries and group karma. In the ethereal plane, greater minds negotiate with world leaders who have passed away. They can help alter the future but only if it is for the good of all. Those who kneel before God like General George Patton did before each battle during World War II, will receive inspiration from the spirit world and help change the course of history. World leaders all have their guides, but few listen.

Past life regression could help even dictators and terrorists shift their thinking. It would alter the world on a massive scale. Hypnotists can regress those who commit evil to get to the karmic root cause and then heal them. Did you know that

Hitler wanted to be a great painter before he became a ruthless dictator, but chose evil over creativity in World War II? If he had pursued art, instead of death and destruction our world would have been a different place today.

I pray for future generations, the abused, the lost, and all the tormented souls on Earth, and I hope you will too.

"The ultimate tragedy is not the oppression and cruelty by the bad people, but the silence over that by good people." — Martin Luther King, Jr.

CHAPTER TEN

THE GODLESS

Did you know that a large percentage of Hollywood movies are financed by China now? Even the new *Barbie* movie was financed by China and has a Chinese map showing they own the China Sea in it. Your children are being controlled by the video hosting company TikTok owned by ByteDance, a Communist Chinese Company, and they compile information on your child and all who join it. Do you want your child's or grandchild's mind controlled by communist propaganda? BEWARE–someday this information may be used to incarcerate you.

Chinese Communist Party and their United States company acquisitions:

Since 1919, Hilton has become a household name throughout the U.S. and other countries. In 2016, HNA

Group, a Chinese aviation and shipping giant, bought a 25% stake for $6.5 billion. This acquisition put two Chinese directors on Hilton's Board of 10.

General Electric covers a wide range of industries, and its appliance division is manufactured in the USA with global parts (and with domestic parts whenever possible). However, in 2016, Chinese investor Haier bought the company's appliance division for $5.4 billion.

While all products are still made in America, the ideas are generated in China. Concern over what the growing amount of U.S. farmland owned by Chinese companies could mean for national security is rising. But what has garnered less attention is the fact that the vast majority—over 80 percent of U.S. farmland owned by Chinese corporations or investors is owned by Smithfield Foods. Located in Smithfield, Virginia, Smithfield was purchased by the Hong Kong-based WH Group for $4.7 billion in 2013. At the time, it was called "the biggest Chinese takeover" of a U.S. corporation, one of the U.S.'s biggest producers of industrial meat.

Anabang Insurance Group, the buyer of this well-known Manhattan hotel, The Waldorf Astoria was unknown in 2014 when it paid nearly $2 billion for the establishment. But it has since become a more common name to investors, buying U.S. insurer Fidelity & Guaranty Life last fall and attempting to buy Starwood Resorts, only to lose out to Marriott at the last minute. Last year Blackstone Group sold its line of luxury hotels to the Chinese company for $3.93 billion (roughly $6 billion, including debt). The deal put Anabang in charge of 16 properties, including assorted Ritz-Carlton locations in California, the Fairmont Scottsdale in Arizona, and the Four Seasons Resort in Jackson Hole, Wyoming.

"League of Legends" is one of the biggest titles in the video game world and is responsible, in part, for the boom in eSports of the past eight years. It's a billion-dollar franchise, but the creator Riot Games started as an independent game developer.

In 2011, though, Chinese holding company Tencent bought a majority stake in Riot for $400 million and in 2015 bought the rest of the company for an undisclosed amount.

Tencent also holds investment stakes in Activision-Blizzard and "Gears of War" creator Epic Games.

Motorola was an early leader in the telecommunications space, dating back to 1928. As mobile devices began to dominate the industry, it spun its handset division off into the independent Motorola Mobility, which was bought by Google in 2012. Two years later, though, the search giant announced it was selling the unit to China-owned Lenovo for $2.9 billion, making Lenovo the world's third-largest smartphone maker.

Popular cinema company AMC, short for American Multi-Cinema, has been around for over a century and is headquartered in Leawood, KS. In 2012, Beijing-based Dalian Wanda Group became the majority stakeholder, giving them the power to make decisions at the executive level. Wanda invested $2.8 billion in the historic deal.

Based in Detroit, Michigan, General Motors is known as America's largest automobile manufacturer. While the company isn't owned by a Chinese company, it relies on its partnership with Shanghai Automotive Industry Corp (SAIC) to stay profitable. In 1998, the two auto giants teamed up to form SAIC-GM, a Chinese brand with a 6 million-square-foot facility in Shanghai.

If that doesn't scare you, it should. Why would the United States allow a communist country to buy our major companies and land? It's a takeover of America from the inside out!

President Biden has been colluding with China and protect them. He allowed a Chinese high-altitude spy balloon to compile sensitive information from our military bases in the U.S. from January 28 to February 4, 2023. The balloon flew across North American airspace, including Alaska, western Canada, and the contiguous United States. On February 4, President Biden finally ordered it shot down by the U.S. Air Force over U.S. territorial waters off the coast of South Carolina. It appears it didn't want to upset the Chinese and the money he and Hunter Biden have received from them.

Amazing how they claim the intel to target Hamas operatives but had no idea the attack on Israel was planned. It was ALLOWED to happen. Israeli civilians sacrificed and now Gaza civilians sacrificed. It is one mass Satanic sacrifice as all 'wars' are. – Best-Selling Author David Icke

CHAPTER ELEVEN

APOCALYPSE NOW

On September 26, 2023, I posted the article below about the recent red auroras seen worldwide as a warning to humanity and predicted that a great war was coming. This morning at 6 a.m. Israeli time, Hamas terrorists launched a murderous surprise attack against the State of Israel on one of its holy days, October 7, killing over 1,400 innocent civilians, men, women, and children, and capturing many on the border of Israel and Palestine. Thousands of Israelis were injured, and Americans were also killed or captured.

A prophecy made on September 23, 2023 by Betsey: In 1927, Jesus reportedly spoke to Lucia, a Carmelite Nun, and the eldest living child of the Fatima Visions that began in May of 1917 and through October 1917. Jesus instructed her to divulge part of the secret given in July 1917, including what the Lady of Fatima had told her regarding five scourges that were to transpire. He said, "When you shall see the night illuminated by an unknown light, know that it is a great sign that God is giving you that He is going to punish the world for its crimes by means of war..."

That sign, as prophesied, came on the night of January 25, 1938, when all of Europe and part of North America was lighted by an extraordinary, brilliant display of the aurora borealis. World War I was the first scourge, and the second was the militant rise of communism and World War II. Lucia said that if the world ignores the Lady's requests, every nation, without exception, will come under Communist domination. Communism is encompassing the world including America.

*In the past two days, brilliant red auroras have appeared over Europe like they did in 1938. Are we being warned of a great conflagration? My answer is a definite YES!

Red Auroras are rare. What makes red auroras rare? Partly it's just that we have trouble seeing them, so they go unreported by sky watchers. Mainly, though, it's because they are the most delicate auroras. Red auroras come from atomic oxygen near the top of Earth's atmosphere. Either oxygen atoms got excited by the solar wind or a CME spit out their red photons very slowly. The radiative lifetime of the transition is 110 seconds–an eternity in the quantum realm. The atoms must remain undisturbed for that long to produce their eerie red light.

As predicted, a CME hit Earth's magnetic field on Sept. 24th (2043 UT). The impact was much stronger than expected. Magnetometer needles in Canada jerked by as much as 129 nT, and a G2-class geomagnetic storm began almost immediately after the CME arrived.

Naked-eye sightings of red auroras are unusual because human eyes are notoriously insensitive to the 6300 Å wavelength of their red light. Yet multiple observers in Scotland and Iceland confirmed that they saw the scarlet glow. Some displays were stunningly red: "These were some of the reddest auroras I've ever seen," says photographer Chris Walker of the Mull of Galloway, Scotland. Red auroras persisted as night fell over North America.

Red auroras over Moray, Scotland, UK on Sept. 24, 2023

Benjamin Netanyahu, Israeli Prime Minister, announced on October 7, 2023, that Israel is in a State of War. Already the United States is involved as the war in the Middle East spreads into Lebanon and Syria. At first President Biden supported the Israeli war on Hamas, then he wanted a cease-fire, and he changed his mind again and now supports Israel. Biden is being pressured by Left Democrats and the major media. The Biden Administration has given billions to Ukraine with no accountability on how money is spent by Zelensky, and now the United States is giving millions to Israel and Palestine. Next China will move on Taiwan, and the U.S. will support Taiwan with millions of dollars. This is the start of World War III as the red auroras in September forewarned.

Conspiracy theorists believe that Biden is afraid that if he stopped funding the Ukraine war, Zelensky would spill the beans about Joe Biden's illegal bribes from Ukraine.

One thing that has puzzled officials and some news reporters is that Israel is known for their great intelligence gathering and has been praised for it, even better than the

United States. How could Hamas run a big tractor through an Israeli fence, drop paragliders into Israel, and attack on foot without the Israeli military knowing? Why didn't the United States intelligence get wind of the attack by Hamas?

Something doesn't sound right about this attack and how it was allowed to happen.

Were the atrocities of innocent women, children, babies, and men allowed to happen to begin a cleansing war on the Palestinian people or ignite World War III? Don't believe everything you hear on the news media and politicians in the coming months and years. An example of fake news happened when an Israeli news station in Israel claimed 40 babies had been decapitated, but it was proven to be false. There were atrocities in Israel by Hamas, and that is true. Yet, the world ran with horrific news without any proof and ignited more hate and anger throughout the world.

Humans are easily manipulated by their emotions, and our handlers know it.

Hamas supporters from colleges and other groups supporting Palestine and Hamas took to the streets in major U.S. cities and throughout the worldwide protesting. Students who are living in the U.S. under a Visa, claimed that the U.S. is evil, but why are they here if they hate the United States? Such a dichotomy. They should be returned to their countries of origin if they feel that way.

Who is right, and who is wrong? Who caused the airstrike?

Meanwhile, President Biden flew to Israel to meet Prime Minister Benjamin Netanyahu, military and other officials in a show of support for Israel, but he didn't denounce Hamas and their slaughter of innocent Israeli people during the trip.

Early nineteenth-century Scottish historian and author Walter Scott (1771-1832) wrote, "*Oh, what a tangled web we weave when first we practice to deceive*! It means that if you tell a lie, you will then have to tell lies to cover up those lies.

Albert Pike's warning of WWIII in 1871

It appears that the Illuminati has been planning World War III since the 1880s.

Few people have ever heard of Albert Pike. He was born December 29, 1809, in Boston, and was the eldest of six children born to Benjamin and Sarah Andrews Pike. He studied at Harvard and later served as a Brigadier-General in the Confederate Army. After the Civil War, Pike was found guilty of treason and jailed, only to be pardoned by fellow freemason President Andrew Johnson on April 22, 1866, who met with him the next day at the White House. On June 20, 1867, Scottish Rite officials conferred upon Johnson the 4th to 32nd freemasonry degrees, and he later went to Boston to dedicate a masonic temple.

Here's another conspiracy theory—Andrew Johnson became the 17th president of the United States after President Abraham Lincoln was assassinated on April 14, 1865. There are stories that Andrew Johnson had Lincoln assassinated to become President. Johnson took the Oath of President on April 15 at 11 a.m., an Illuminati number.

On November 22, 1963, President John F. Kennedy was assassinated in Dallas, Texas. Lyndon B. Johnson, a freemason, took the Oath on Airforce One at 2:38 p.m. CST, a number that totaled 13, another Illuminati number. Stories persist today that LJB was involved with Kennedy's assassination to continue the Illuminati plan.

Both Andrew Johnson and Lyndon B. Johnson were Freemasons. Both presidents' successors were named Johnson. Andrew Johnson was born in 1808, and Lyndon Johnson was born in 1908. Both presidents, Lincoln and Kennedy were shot in the head on a Friday. What are the odds? It was planned to change the outcome of history.

Pike was a 33rd Degree Freemason, and he was the head of the ancient accepted Scottish Rite of freemasonry, being the Grand Commander of North American freemasonry from 1859 and retaining the position until he died in 1891. In 1869, he was a top leader in the Knights of the Ku Klux Klan and also a member of the Knights of the Golden Circle/Sons of Liberty. Pike was also a satanist, who indulged in the occult, and he possessed a bracelet which he used to summon Lucifer, with whom he communicated.

The following are extracts from the letter, showing how

three world wars have been planned for many generations:

"The first world war must be brought about to permit the Illuminati to overthrow the power of the czars in Russia and make that country a fortress of atheistic communism. the divergences caused by the "Agentur" [agents] of the Illuminati between the British and Germanic empires will be used to foment this war. at the end of the war, communism will be built and used to destroy the other governments and to weaken religions.

"The second world war must be fomented by taking advantage of the differences between the fascists and the political Zionists. this war must be brought about so that Nazism is destroyed and that the political Zionism be strong enough to institute a sovereign state of Israel in Palestine. During the second world war, international communism must become strong enough to balance Christendom, which would be then restrained and held in check until the time when we would need it for the final social cataclysm.

"The third world war must be fomented by taking advantage of the differences caused by "Agentur" of the "Illuminati" between the political Zionists and the leaders of the Islamic world. the war must be conducted in such a way that Islam (the Moslem Arabic world) and political Zionism (the State of Israel) mutually destroy each other.

“Meanwhile the other nations, once more divided on this issue will be constrained to fight to the point of complete physical, moral, spiritual, and economic exhaustion...we shall unleash the nihilists and the atheists, and we shall provoke a formidable social cataclysm which in all its horror will show clearly to the nations the effect of absolute atheism, the origin of savagery and the most bloody turmoil.

“Then everywhere, the citizens, obliged to defend themselves against the world minority of revolutionaries, will exterminate those destroyers of civilization, and the multitude, disillusioned with Christianity, whose deistic spirits will from that moment be without compass or direction, anxious for an ideal, but without knowing where to render adoration, will receive the true light through the universal manifestation of the pure doctrine of Lucifer, brought finally out in public view.

"This manifestation will result from the general reactionary movement which will follow the destruction of Christianity and atheism, both conquered and exterminated at the same time."

This is what is believed to be the letter of Albert Pike, a Freemason and Satanist, to Giuseppe Mazzini, and the letter is said to have been in the British Museum Library in London until 1977.

This is the Illuminati's evil plan for humanity!

To die with hatred for any cause or people, or for any reason, is a great disadvantage. The problem of war will sooner or later teach you that when you kill another human, basically you will end up killing yourself. How can an eye for an eye ever end? As Gandhi said, "An eye for an eye makes the whole world blind." The destructive cycle will go on forever, and no one will be victorious. The deaths of millions will create a karmic effect on cities, towns, states, regions, and countries, and eventually karma will be met.

The United States is involved now in two proxy wars—Ukraine and Israel. A proxy war occurs when a major power instigates or plays a major role in supporting and directing a party to a conflict but does only a small portion of the actual fighting itself. And that's what is happening now as the United States enters into the Ukraine war with limited troops and in Israel.

The lyrics to the song *War* were written in 1970 by Edwin Starr. Although the song applied to the Vietnam War, it applies today.

War, huh, yeah
What is it good for?
Absolutely nothing, uh-huh, uh-huh
War, huh, yeah
What is it good for?
Absolutely nothing, say it again, y'all
War, huh, good God
What is it good for?
Absolutely nothing, listen to me
Oh war, I despise

'Cause it means destruction of innocent lives—War means tears to thousands of mothers' eyes
When their sons go off to fight and lose their lives
I said, war, huh, good God, y'all
What is it good for?
Absolutely nothing, say it again
War, huh, whoa-oh-whoa-oh, Lord
What is it good for?
Absolutely nothing, listen to me
War, it ain't nothing but a heartbreak
War, friend only to the undertaker
Oh, war, is an enemy to all mankind
The thought of war blows my mind
War has caused unrest within the younger generation
Induction then destruction, who wants to die?
Oh, war, huh, good God, y'all
What is it good for?
Absolutely nothing, say it, say it, say it
War, huh, uh-huh, yeah, uh
What is it good for?
Absolutely nothing, listen to me
War, it ain't nothing but a heartbreaker
War, it got one friend, that's the undertaker
Oh, war has shattered many a young man's dreams
Made him disabled, bitter, and mean
Life is much too short and precious to spend fighting wars these days
War can't give life, it can only take it away
Oh, war, huh, good God, y'all
What is it good for?
Absolutely nothing, say it again
War, huh, whoa-oh-whoa-oh, Lord
What is it good for?
Absolutely nothing, listen to me
War, it ain't nothing but a heartbreaker
War, friend only to the undertaker
Peace, love, and understanding, tell me
Is there no place for them today?
They say we must fight to keep our freedom

But lord knows there's got to be a better way
Oh, war, huh, good God, y'all
What is it good for?
You tell me, (nothing) say it, say it, say it, say it
War, huh, good God, yeah, huh

CHAPTER TWELVE

CLIMATE CHANGE HOAX

There's no climate emergency but you are being conned to believe that malarky by people like Climate Change Czar John Kerry who flies around the world in his private jet. The alarmist message pushed by global elites is purely political, and to make you buy electric cars and go green on everything. That's what 1,609 scientists and informed professionals stated when they signed the Global Climate Intelligence Group's "World Climate Declaration."

Biden's attempt to push wind turbines into the ocean and on land is failing. The company that started electric school buses is now bankrupt. Electric cars will sit on car lots unsold.

A slew of canceled offshore wind projects and contracts have jeopardized the Biden administration's push to expand the new industry and its promise of clean power for coastal states. The latest setback came Tuesday night when the Danish developer Orsted said it is scrapping two large projects off the southern coast of New Jersey. Ocean Wind 1 and 2 became too expensive because of rising interest rates and competition for limited supplies and equipment, the company said. The projects had also become a hot-button political issue, with local grass-roots opposition and campaigns tied to fossil-fuel interests. The Biden administration had planned an expansion to generate 30 gigawatts of offshore wind power by the end of the decade—projects that could not be undone by future administrations. Biden's baloney climate and green energy will go bye-bye and save whales, birds, and fish that have been killed by wind turbines. Eventually, wind turbines will disappear as a detrimental energy for the environment.

The following article was published in the Epoch Times.

"Climate science should be less political, while climate policies should be more scientific," the declaration begins. "Scientists should openly address uncertainties and exaggerations in their predictions of global warming, while politicians should dispassionately count the real costs as well as the imagined benefits of their policy measures."

The group is an independent "climate watchdog" founded in 2019 by emeritus professor of geophysics Guus Berkhout and science journalist Marcel Crok. According to the group's website, its objective is to "generate knowledge and understanding of the causes and effects of climate change as well as the effects of climate policy." And it does so by objectively looking at the facts and engaging in scientific research into climate change and climate policy.

The declaration's signatories include Nobel Laureates, theoretical physicists, meteorologists, professors, and environmental scientists worldwide. And when a select few were asked by The Epoch Times why they signed the declaration stating that the "climate emergency" is a farce, they all stated a variation of "because it's true."

"I signed the declaration because I believe the climate is no longer studied scientifically. Rather, it has become an item of faith," Haym Benaroya, a distinguished professor of mechanical and aerospace engineering at Rutgers University, told The Epoch Times. "The earth has warmed about 2 degrees F since the end of the Little Ice Age around 1850, but that hardly constitutes an emergency—or even a crisis—since the planet has been warmer yet over the last few millennia," Ralph Alexander, a retired physicist and author of the website "Science Under Attack," told The Epoch Times.

"There is plenty of evidence that average temperatures were higher during the so-called Medieval Warm Period (centered around the year 1000), the Roman Warm Period (when grapes and citrus fruits were grown in now much colder Britain), and in the early Holocene (after the last regular Ice Age ended)." The climate emergency is "fiction," he said unequivocally.

Science is based on observational evidence, together with logic, to make sense of the evidence. Very little, if any, evidence exists that human emissions of CO2 cause rising temperatures. There is a correlation between the two, but the correlation isn't particularly strong: The Earth cooled, for example, from about 1940 to 1970, while the atmospheric CO2 level continued to go up. Computer climate models are all that connects global warming to CO2."

When asked why CO2 was singled out as the cause of the climate emergency, Mr. Alexander said it goes back to James Hansen, an astrophysicist and the head of NASA's Goddard Institute for Space Studies from 1981 to 2013, and an ardent environmentalist.

"The chances of CO2 being the number one culprit are very slim. CO2 undoubtedly contributes, but there are several natural cycles that most likely do, too," he said. "These include solar variability and ocean cycles, both ignored in climate models—because we don't know how to incorporate them—or represented poorly. While climate activists will tell you otherwise, climate science is still in its infancy, and there is a great deal we don't yet understand about our climate."

He said one example is a recent research paper that estimated that changes in the sun's output could explain 70 to 80 percent of global warming. Research such as that doesn't gain much traction because the IPCC is committed to the idea that human CO2 is the cause of global warming.

The Elites want you to believe our world should be all electric, but suppose a huge solar eruption takes place and a CME hits Earth knocking out the entire energy grid worldwide. What then? There would be no gas to warm your house or cook on. Your electric car would not start. The greatest polluters in the world are China and India, and if you think they are going to go all-electric, dream on!

President Biden, John Kerry, and others won't give up their private jets that burn around 5,000 gallons of fuel per hour. That's the equivalent of about 400 passenger cars. The average commercial jet burns about half that much. What hypocrites!

President Biden wants everyone to buy expensive electric cars by 2035 that still have exploding issues under certain conditions. If a car gets caught in a flood This can lead to an event called "thermal runaway," in which the heat propagates from one cell to the next, causing them to burn. In a small number of cases when an EV is submerged in water, contaminants or salt in the water can cause short-circuiting, especially after the water drains from the battery.

Many of the auto workers will need new jobs if auto companies are forced to make mostly electric cars. AI will replace humans in the future.

Where are those Earth crusaders like Green Peace who were going to save the Earth's environment? Both solar panels covering the countryside and wind turbines are eye sores that don't produce enough energy to exist. It's all a joke for the consumer.

So please young people stop destroying precious art, gluing yourselves to walls and art, and blocking roads and highways, because you believe it will make a difference with "Climate Change." But how can it be if Climate Change doesn't exist? You've got to wake up to how you are being manipulated by the Family of Dark.

Cleaning up Earth

There are technologies that could clean up Earth very quickly if that were the plan. But since earthlings don't take responsibility for Earth, there would be no point. We must first learn to honor our world. We must learn to honor our bodies and realize that without Earth we would not be here. Our bodies and our planet are the two greatest gifts we have. If each of you took time to express sacredness, honor, cherish, and love Earth, and your physical body, everything would change on this beautiful planet. Look at how most people treat their bodies. Most are hugely obese and eat horrible toxic food. Everyone wants convenient food that has little or no nutritional value. You might as well put cardboard in your hamburger bun to get the same zero nutritional value.

Earth is more resilient than you can imagine. It is here to feed you and sustain you. The animals are also here to work in cooperation with humans. If everything was done in love, it would have the force of the Creator behind it. Done with love, there would be no hurt and no harm. Ask yourself: "Am I operating with my highest integrity? Am I operating with love? Is the love frequency my intention for Earth, and the creatures, and people that I encounter?"

During the 1990s, I spent a lot of time connecting with Native Americans throughout the West, and I loved their pow-wow ceremonies, the chanting, and the drumming like Mother Earth's heartbeat. Sage bundles permeated the air to cleanse the sweat lodge as we prayed and communicated with the Great Spirit and all the other spirits around us.

In 1993, I organized a sweat lodge ceremony and Vision Quest in Sun Valley, Idaho. My friend and mentor Ed McGaa, Eagle Man, an Oglala Sioux ceremonial leader officiated the sweat lodge ceremony, saying prayers in his native language and blessing all twenty-five of us with Native American Names. I was "Rainbow Shield Woman".

Ed called on the four directions as the lava glowed in the fire pit. The four winds carry the life blood out of the lodge to the four quarters of our planet. Our lifeblood seeped back into

Earth Mother. The peace pipe was passed around to the participants. Each one received a blessing, our lifeblood, and our breath carried throughout the cosmos. It was a powerful ceremony.

Indigenous people honor everything on Earth. If they take something from Earth, they give something back. They pray for animals taken for their food. Can you imagine beings who do this in love and the highest integrity for the living being on Earth? Remember in the *Wizard of Oz* movie where Dorothy walked into the enchanted forest with her Oz friends and picked an apple off a tree on their way to the Emerald City? The tree suddenly slaps Dorothy's hand and says, "Well, how would you like to have someone come along and pick something off of you?"

Although trees can speak, they are living beings and should be honored as such.

People will have the courage to speak up and stand up again when they have nothing to lose. When enough people create their own reality—*consciously create it*—you will create a new planet. It will be the hundredth monkey effect. The hundredth monkey effect is a hypothetical phenomenon in which a new behavior or idea is spread rapidly by unexplained means from one group to all related groups once a critical number of members of one group exhibit the new behavior or acknowledge the new idea. The behavior was said to propagate even to groups that are physically separated and have no apparent means of communicating with each other.

There will be shocking revelations in the coming decade as Earth collides with many dimensions and probabilities. Some of these realities will be shocking. There is no one reality and each human branches off into other realities continuously through your thoughts. You change the world you occupy at the moment. There are, and always have been probable Earths and probable experiences. There are probably "you's" leading quite different lives than the ones you know now. You are energy and frequency, but most haven't figured that out yet. Even when you pass over, you become pure energy and your thoughts create your ethereal plane. If you want heaven, you can create that too but if you believe you are unworthy of heaven, it won't exist. Neither place exists. You can travel the Cosmos, visit galaxies, other planets, and other worlds. You can visit family and friends in the spirit world.

Have you experienced the *Mandela Effect* where you are positive a certain event happened but didn't or a certain celebrity died, when in fact that person is still alive? That's known as a time shift.

CHAPTER THIRTEEN

QUALITY OF LIFE

When humans make the quality of life the number one priority in their lives by honoring the quality of Earth's life, there will be very few Earth changes upon this planet. However, more humans, particularly in the Western world, are concerned with a very different quality of life: how many electronic devices they own, who they can impress on social media, how many clothes are in their closets, and how many cars are in their garages. They are not connected to the side effects of material manufacturing on the sentient being that we call Earth.

If humans do not change—if they do not make the shift in values and realize that without Earth they could not be here, then Mother Earth, in her love for her own initiation and her reaching a higher frequency, will bring about a cleansing, that will balance the planet once again. There is the potential for many people to leave the planet within a day. If such a cataclysmic event took place on Earth, maybe people would begin to wake up to what is going on. There must be global change immediately.

How willing are you to change? When you change your life, you automatically make the change available to the entire planet. Earth feels deprived of her integrity, dishonored, and unloved. She is a living organism. If you don't love yourself and honor yourself and your body, it affects Earth. Our thought frequency is that powerful.

Earth is more resilient than you can ever imagine. She is here to feed you and sustain you. The animals are also here to work in cooperation with you. If everything is done with love, it has the force of the Creator behind it.

At this time, many people do not want to put themselves on the line and speak out with integrity because they are afraid of being shunned or losing their jobs. One of the most incredible things that can happen in any civilization is when everyone's security is threatened, humans suddenly begin to stand up to those who want to control you.

When enough people create their own reality in *mass* consciousness, you will create a new world. There will be a splitting of worlds. We, together, will change the world we occupy. It is constructed of energy, and that energy frequency takes form through the thoughts and minds of those who participate in the world.

You have heard the predictions of Earth changes over and over, and some of you believe it couldn't happen where you live or that you could one day wake up in a civil war or world war. You probably think events like that happen to others in another part of the globe but not to you. What if the changes happen at your doorstep or in the next city near you? What about the major cities collapsing either from an earthquake or by decay from crime, homelessness, drugs, and thousands upon thousands of illegal migrants who won't be able to find work and will need to depend on the government for aid?

Watch what happens when winter arrives and the millions of illegals who crossed over our U.S. borders experience their first harsh winters of snow and extreme cold, causing some to freeze to death. They can't survive in tents and most don't have clothing to keep them warm. Will they come for your possessions, your house, apartment or condo, your food, your money, and force you to leave or kill you if you try to stop them?

The way events are unfolding now it could happen to the United States of America.

What happens when you awake someday to find that there was a huge tear in the Earth from New York City to Washington, D.C.? That tear is called the New Madrid seismic zone that would cause major destruction in Missouri, northeastern Arkansas, western Tennessee, western Kentucky, and southern Illinois. It would also rock Washington, D.C., and New York. Would this shake up your world to awaken you a little bit? Would it be enough to restructure and revalue your lives?

Unfortunately, there are those who care little about others, and would rob, loot, and take what they think is owed to them. They would even kill. Can you defend yourself? Biden wants to your guns and to outlaw bows and arrows. How will you defend yourselves?

When Earth does shift, not everyone will experience the same thing. Those who need to experience destruction will experience an Earth shift or rotation with destruction because they will not fit within the new frequency. Those who are prepared to hold a higher vibration will experience a frequency shift. So, for some, it will be the end of their lives as they know it and dire destruction, while for others, they will experience a state of ecstasy. All potentials exist. Remember that you live in a symbolic and vibrational world that is the result of your thoughts.

CHAPTER FOURTEEN

SUPERNOVA

According to recent UK Crop Circles interpreted by Red Collie on his Crop Circle Connector website, he said that a star is about to do something. I predicted two years ago that Supergiant Star Betelgeuse would go Supernova sometime in the next few years. In May and June 2023, its brightness increased by almost 50 percent, which means it can be classed as a variable star. Betelgeuse's recent behavior has led scientists to conclude that the star might have entered its final life stage and go supernova very soon.

A team of astronomers led by Hideyuki Saio (Tohoku University) finds that Betelgeuse has puffed up far larger than previously thought, more than 1200 times wider than the sun. This means the giant star may be running out of carbon fuel.

"After carbon is exhausted in the core, a core-collapse leading to a supernova explosion is expected," write the authors.

This fiery demise will be a spectacular sight for observers on Earth. Since the star is only 650 light-years from Earth, those layers of gas and dust will shine as bright as the full moon in our sky for several weeks.

Betelgeuse is undoubtedly a red giant star that has already burned through its primary fuel hydrogen and is now fusing helium in its core into heavier elements. The point at which a star runs out of hydrogen in its lifetime is unmissable. Stars short on hydrogen need to put extra energy into igniting the helium produced during the fusion of hydrogen, which forces them to expand dozens of times beyond their original size. In the process, they also become cooler and redder.

Astronomers know that Betelgeuse is huge. If it were to sit at the center of our solar system, the scorching gas in its outer atmosphere would reach far enough to engulf even the planet Jupiter. However, the exact width of Betelgeuse is hard to measure. That's because instead of being one rather smooth ball of plasma, Betelgeuse is a lumpy clump of boiling gas bubbles shrouded in burped-out dust clouds. To measure its diameter is therefore not easy yet and the case for determining Betelgeuse's remaining lifetime rests on the star's size.

In a new controversial study, a team of astronomers led by Hideyuki Saio from the Tohoku University in Japan suggests that Betelgeuse is larger than what most researchers believe. This could be possible as Betelgeuse is known to pulsate—expand and shrink, dim, and brighten up at regular intervals. Most obviously, Betelgeuse's brightness swings up and down every 420 days. Astronomers attribute this brightening to the periodical expansion of the star's envelope, or roughly spherical outer region, in a phenomenon known as the fundamental mode.

There are other quirks in Betelgeuse's behavior, also appearing regularly, which astronomers attribute to additional turbulent processes taking place inside the dying star. One of those additional variations takes place on a 2,200-day cycle, and astronomers have no explanation for it. The team led by Saio proposed that this 2,200-day oscillation could represent Betelgeuse's main pulsation mode while the 420-day brightness variation could be a secondary quirk.

Such a scenario, however, requires Betelgeuse to be up to one-third wider for these models of its evolution to work, Saio told *Space.com* in an email.

But for Betelgeuse to be as wide as the models require, it would also have to be in a later stage of its life, already done burning helium and instead running on carbon, which arose from the previous fusion of helium atoms. Whether a red giant star is burning helium or carbon makes a big difference in terms of how much life it has left. The helium-burning phase of a red giant star's life lasts tens of thousands of years. When carbon-burning switches on, the end is nigh, at least in cosmic terms, and might come within a few thousand years.

"Although we cannot determine exactly how much carbon remains right now, our evolution models suggest that the carbon exhaustion would occur in less than 300 years," Saio wrote. "After the carbon exhaustion, fusions of further heavier elements would occur in probably a few tens of years, and after that the central part would collapse and a supernova explosion would occur."

Such an event would excite skywatchers worldwide. The last time a nearby star went supernova was in 1604. Although stars explode somewhere in the universe daily, most of them are too far away to be visible without powerful telescopes. Betelgeuse, on the contrary, despite its regular pulsations, has been a fixture in the top ten brightest stars of our sky for at least the past 100 years.

Two crop circles appeared at Chillingham Lane, near Winchester, Hampshire on July 4, 2023, in the same field.

Two new crop circles on the same day and in the same field certainly had a similar message. By bringing together a star and an emanation of energy (or light) in waves, we can be faced with the warning of a new star in the sky, or the star Betelgeuse, which always surprises astronomers with its sudden changes in luminosity, which could shine, for the last time, as a supernova at any time. When two crop circles appear on the same day and in the same field, it is evident that their messages must be interpreted within a set. The board, laid out in the direction of a diamond (inverted square) has nine clear layers, and the first image that comes is of light waves propagating from an energy center.

This might portend the existence of an object approaching Earth and the theory of the second Sun, Nemesis, the brown dwarf, Planet X whose motion interferes with the Sun's energy stability.

In the past few months, photographs and videos of two suns have been posted on social media. The photograph below was taken in Los Angels as the sun was setting sometime in August.

Planet X aka Nibiru is passing through our solar system and its magnetic pull is causing extreme weather throughout the world. Will it's pull be strong enough to cause the Earth's poles to shift as the late great psychic Edgar Cayce predicted in a trance-like state in 1940?

Legends persist that once the sun rose in the West and set in the East. Preserved Mammoths in Siberia have been discovered with undigested food in their mouths frozen instantly by some great cataclysm. Their bodies didn't have time to decompose. The grass and flowers in their stomachs show they lived in a temperate climate. Antarctic core samples show that the current South Pole once had a temperate climate as well.

Scientists don't know what caused the great shift. However, the typical estimates suggest that 50% or more of all-star systems are binary systems. Then what happened to our Sun's twin? It travels through our solar system every 3,657 years. Planet X is a dark unlit star, known as a "brown dwarf," and it is difficult to see next to the sun. Most photographs of this camera-shy solar twin are caught as the sun is rising or setting in the west.

Where's the evidence of a pole shift?

The discovery of fossil whale bones in Michigan has been a source of some embarrassment for the conventional geologic story of the history of the Great Lakes region, and the notion that the area has remained above sea level for 290 million years since the end of the Pennsylvanian period, as whale fossils are evidence that the land was submerged beneath the sea. The bones were found at 440 feet, 500, and 600 feet above sea level. The whole ocean was on the move during a pole shift is the best explanation for such strange discoveries.

It is known that sheer cliff faces are created when rock is torn and thrust upwards with unimaginable force, caused by a pole shift. Coastlines sank beneath the sea and are redefined as land stretched apart. The sunken forest of New Hampshire is visible at low tide on Jenness Beach, but what happened to cause the event if it was from a pole shift?

Ancient cities have been discovered that were inundated on coasts and other man-made structures found beneath the waves have also been found all around the world. For example, the Bimini Road in the Bahamas and the nearby remains of a harbor wall are now submerged. The Yonaguni Monument found submerged south of Okinaw, Japan appears man-made. The Yonaguni Monument, also known as "Yonaguni Submarine Ruins", is a submerged rock formation off the coast of Yonaguni, the southernmost of the Ryukyu Islands, in Japan. It lies approximately 100 kilometers east of Taiwan. Marine geologist Masaaki Kimura claims that the formations are man-made stepped monoliths.

The Yonaguni Monument

Ancient stories abound of massive floods that covered Earth. Even the Bible tells how God warned Noah that a catastrophic flood would encompass the world. He was instructed to build an ark for his family and every species on the Earth. Noah and his ark survived the great flood. Finally, the waters subsided 150 days later, and the Ark came to rest on the mountains of Ararat, in the region of Turkey.

Ice Ages, like the last one in Western Europe, ended approximately 10,000 years ago, showing us the times when the North Pole was further south. Scientists have tried to explain the drastic drop in temperature by claiming the Earth moved further away from the Sun in its orbit for a brief time. But this explanation doesn't make sense when you consider that France was under ice while Siberia at the same latitude had no ice at all.

There are signs of ancient settlements that existed worldwide but were deserted long ago, like pyramids found in China, Bosnia, Franch, South America, and Egypt. Numerous Maya ruins have been found in the jungles of South America that were suddenly abandoned due to abrupt changes in the climate. People were forced to migrate to find better living conditions, leaving their massive stone structures in the jungle.

The Indus Valley civilization thrived for 2,000 years spanned over eight thousand years, and then died out suddenly and completely around 1700 B.C., the time of the last pole shift.

CHAPTER FIFTEEN

EXTREME WEATHER

June through August 2023 marked the world's hottest three-month period in recorded history, and the average global temperature in July was more than 2°F (1.1°C) hotter than last century's average, according to the United States' National Oceanic and Atmospheric Administration (NOAA). Humans are not responsible for the crazy weather Earth is experiencing now. So far in 2023, there have been 23 confirmed weather disasters with losses exceeding $1 billion each in the United States.

June was the hottest month ever charted on the planet in at least 125,000 years. "We have never seen anything like this before," said Carlo Buontempo, director of Europe's Copernicus Climate Change Service.

Antarctic sea ice, meanwhile, reached its lowest June extent since the dawn of the satellite era, at 17 percent below the 1991-2020 average, Copernicus said. The previous record, set a year earlier, was about 9 percent below average.

In the summer of 2023, Earth experienced weather extremes that included record-breaking heat waves in China, where Beijing surpassed 40 degrees Celsius (104 degrees Fahrenheit) for the first time, and in Mexico and Texas, where officials were once again struggling to keep the electricity grid up and running.

It's not just that records are being broken—but the massive margins with which conditions are surpassing previous extremes, scientists note. In parts of the North Atlantic, temperatures are running as high as 9 degrees Fahrenheit above normal, the warmest observed there in more than 170 years. The warm waters helped northwestern Europe, including the United Kingdom, clinch its warmest June on record.

The wildfire smoke that repeatedly choked parts of the United States this summer is a visible reminder of abnormal spring heat and unusually dry weather that have fueled an unprecedented wildfire season in Canada, which saw both its hottest May and June. Canada had wildfires that began in March 2023 and grew in June and spread across all 13 provinces. Some fires are still burning in Canada. The provinces and territories affected included Alberta, British Columbia, the Northwest Territories, Nova Scotia, Ontario, and Quebec. Smoke covered large areas of the eastern United States for weeks and eventually moved into Florida. Even the Northwest was covered in smoke for several days.

In early August 2023, a series of wildfires, referred to as the Hawaii Firestorm by the United States government, broke out on the island of Maui. Maui experienced the most horrible wildfire ever recorded due to winds from a hurricane off the coast. People were never alerted to the danger, and roads were blocked, keeping people held in the danger zones. It is estimated that 115 people, as well as animals, perished in the wildfire that destroyed Lahaina.

Part of it was negligence by the electric company who didn't turn off the electricity, and the stupid authorities cut off the water supply, so fires couldn't be extinguished. It was a perfect storm of incompetence.

On August 30, Hurricane Idalia hit Florida at 125 mph as a Category 3 and did major damage to the coast and homes, but because of Governor Ron DeSantis's quick actions, people were saved or moved away from the hurricane's path. Only 10 people died.

Is Climate Change due to human neglect or fossil fuels? Could it be from Planet X moving through our solar system and pulling on the Earth's magnetic field? Earth goes through many changes, and Planet X has been the culprit of the polar shifts.

Winter 2023 and 2024 Weather

The coming winter will bring endless snow and rain to the Northwest. The Northwest and Northern California will have heavy snow this year and the Midwest and Eastern United States will shiver from extreme cold for the Arctic Express. Expect extreme floods and storms in Europe and droughts and fires in other regions. The Southwest United States will be dry until spring and by late summer heavy monsoon rains will bring flash floods.

What is causing increased weather extremes on the planet? Surely, not fossil fuels, humans, or anything related to humans. Sure, we've harmed the Earth and the waters on Earth, but humans aren't causing weather conditions like we will experience in 2023. Even if our gas-powered automobiles, gas stoves, and heaters are taken away, that won't transform Earth's weather, not even for the Elites.

Scientists say the evidence supports the idea that one or more "super-Earths"—planets up to 10 times more massive than Earth may orbit far beyond Neptune. These bodies would be too far and dim to have shown up in any existing telescope, but future observatories may be able to spot them if they are out there.

As I explained earlier, Planet X is entering our solar system now as more and more people capture two suns on their cell phones. Earth's weather is going to get more extreme in 2024 and 2025 caused by what the Biden Administration calls

"Climate Change." They will try to convince us that we must cut back on wasteful energy while they continue to fly in their private gas-consuming jets and consume lots of energy in their huge expensive mansions. What a farce!

Countdown to Earth shifting

When Venus and the Dark Twin escape from the cup, the particle crowding is suddenly eased, allowing Planet X to come forward toward the Earth. The Earth's first evasion is to tilt her N Pole away from the oncoming Planet X to such a degree, and so violently, that she leans over to the left and then *rebounds* as a reaction to the right. This is the severe wobble, for a length of 9 days, as a recent crop circle has depicted. Finally, the rebound is repressed, for a lingering lean to the left of 4.5 days or so. Then a progression where the North Pole of Earth is pushed away from the Sun and approaching Planet X, until the point where 3 days of darkness is unmistakable, depending on which hemisphere you live on. This progression is another 2-3 days in time. Then the 3 days of darkness and the 6 days of sunrise west, which is a momentum and turnaround for the swing into the 3 days of darkness.

Then the Earth rights herself, side by side with Planet X, and begins her rotation slowdown. It is during this time that the Earth is drawn toward Planet X so that Planet X quickly increases in size in the skies and is the writhing monster of legend seen by all. Slowing rotation is not a linear matter, but exponential as the Earth is pulled closer to Planet X. The Earth moans, groans, and complains as the core pulls at the crust but the crust is gripped, increasingly, and held by Planet X.

The Earth's slowing is a lurching matter too. When the Atlantic Rift is exposed, the grip slows the rotation, but when hidden, rotation tries to return which causes earthquakes and stretch zone accidents. Hurricane winds will sweep across the globe, tsunamis will inundate coastal cities, mega earthquakes will shake the land and volcanoes will awaken. Violent weather will persist for days. There will be increased meteor showers.

The exact position of the Earth when it stops rotation can't be calculated yet, and what shores will experience the worst tidal waves can't be predicted. Stay clear of recently active volcanoes, but old ones can erupt. Remove yourselves from areas where mountain building is likely to occur. Flat plains or plateaus are the safest.

Cities will not be a place to be when the poles shift to heavy earthquake damage and violent looters. Escape routes will be blocked, bridges will fall or be damaged. Earthquakes could measure over 9.0 on the Richter Scale.

Boil all water for at least 20 minutes. Learn what plants are edible and what plants are poisonous.

Emergency management teams will be beyond exhaustion, government services are in disarray, and travel has become almost impossible. Don't depend on FEMA to help! You are on your own to survive after the planet settles down. The Elite will run to their massive bunkers well hidden worldwide. They could risk being buried in their bunkers under feet of earth without any way to escape.

We can only pray that a horrific polar shift or nuclear bomb detonation will never happen.

CHAPTER SIXTEEN

MACGREGOR'S PROPHECY

Retired US Army Colonel Douglas Macgregor, a decorated combat veteran, author of five books, a Ph.D., and a Defense and Foreign Policy consultant, has been covering the Psyop-Ukraine-invasion with uncanny accuracy and insight.

Recently, he appeared on the PBD Podcast, and made what may just be his most dystopian prediction to date:

I don't think we'll ever get to the 2024 election. I think things are going to implode in Washington before then. I think our economic financial condition is fragile – it's going to come home to roost in ugly ways.

Now I will tell you I don't know exactly how it will happen, but I think we're going to end up in a situation where we find out the banks are closed for two or three weeks, and nobody can get into them.

I think we're going to run into something like that. I also think that the levels of violence and criminality in our cities is so high that it's going to spill over into other places in society.

People that normally think they can live remote from the problem are now beginning to be touched by the problem. Then I look at this thing in Ukraine.

I think Ukraine is going to lose catastrophically – it's going to be a complete collapse and that too is going to have an effect here at home because people are going to say, well, wait a minute everybody told us Ukraine was winning, everybody told us X Y and Z.

I mean the Russian hoax is on steroids. All of those things are going to come together or converge in some way that's going to prevent us from reaching you know the status quo. Oh. Another election... Oh, another set of campaigns... And so forth... And when the One World Government that manufactured all of these very problems *swoops in to offer their* "solutions" *upon the banks reopening and the power grid going back online, what will the populace that just went through yet another round of mass-induced fear acquiesce to?*

France is quite literally burning as a result of the globalists' importation of replacement migration invaders. These weaponized "refugees" were relocated for the sole purpose of obliterating the status quo, and creating a permanent state of violent destabilization. At this rate, France will never have another election again. And the only thing preventing this from happening in America is the 2nd Amendment, and so the "Biden" regime needs to manufacture another kind of event, or series of events (i.e. psyops), in order to disrupt the upcoming election.

We are now quite literally in the middle innings of the Great Reset.

When do We the People finally stop reacting to the various psyops, and start to push back hard with total nonviolent noncompliance? Whatever they attempt to foist upon us next, do not get demoralized, do not get depressed, do not despair.

Good always defeats evil in the end.

On October 20, 2023, Macgregor warned that the U.S. military is on the brink of sparking "Armageddon." In an opinion Newsweek article titled "Avoiding Armageddon," published by *The American Conservative* earlier this week, Macgregor argued that "the stage is now set for a battle of annihilation" in the ongoing Israeli-Palestinian conflict. He warned that the U.S. was "poised to stumble into the conflict" and urged President Joe Biden to break with "the ruling political class in Washington" and support a ceasefire.

CHAPTER SEVENTEEN

TIME TRAVEL EXISTS

I've always known that time travel exists, and Albert Einstein believed it too. His theories of relativity stated that an object moving at the speed of light will be able to travel into the future, but only time travel into the future, and not into the past.

Probably one of the strangest stories of time travel reportedly happened around October 28, 1943, during World War II to the U.S. Navy destroyer escort U.S.S. Eldridge in the Philadelphia Naval Shipyard in Philadelphia, Pennsylvania. Conspiracy theorists claim the U.S.S. Eldridge was part of a top-secret experiment dubbed "Project Rainbow" to render the ship invisible to enemy radar or create an illusion of total optical invisibility. Many regard the story as a hoax and the Navy maintains no such experiment occurred, but there are some indications the story may well have had validity.

The experiment was based on the unified field theory, a term coined by Albert Einstein. There were even rumors that the genius inventor and mechanical and electrical engineer Nikola Tesla's experiments were involved. The test reportedly used the generation of an intense magnetic field around the ship, which would refract or bend light or radar waves around the ship, like a mirage created on a hot summer day. Legend claims the experiment was a success except that the ship physically disappeared for a time and then returned. But something went drastically wrong for the men on board.

The U.S. Navy released the U.S.S. Eldridge's deck log and war diary, which clearly showed the ship was headed to New York on October 18 and remained there until November 1. But this event could certainly have been a cover-up, which the U.S. government and U.S. military have been known to do because of national security. Before that fateful October day, several tests were conducted on the Eldridge.

It was a June day in 1943 that the U.S.S. Eldridge was fitted with tons of experimental electronic equipment—two massive generators of 75 KVA each, three RF transmitters mounted on the deck, three thousand "6L6" power amplifier tubes and more hardware to generate massive electromagnetic fields to bend light and radio waves around the ship. Then on July 22, 1943, the generators were turned on, and the electromagnetic field started to build, creating a strange greenish fog around the ship. Suddenly the fog disappeared and so did the U.S.S. Eldridge. The scientific team and U.S. Navy officers were thrilled by their great achievement: the ship and crew had vanished from radar and were completely invisible to the eyes. Slowly the fog returned along with the ship, but with one terrible exception. When the ship was boarded by elite officers and scientists, they found men on deck roaming around, disoriented and sick to their stomachs.

The next test was conducted on October 28, 1943, when the electromagnetic field generators were turned on, and again the Eldridge vanished. Everything seemed to be going well until the ship vanished in a blinding blue flash. Within seconds the Eldridge was transported to Norfolk, Virginia, over 200 miles away, and then materialized back in the Philadelphia Naval Yard. This time the side effects were worse: men screaming in agony physically fused to bulkheads, others went insane, and some vanished totally or ended up momentarily in another location. The men who survived were never the same again. Those who did live through the ordeal were discharged as "mentally unfit" for duty, regardless of their true condition.

The ship was transported across space and time where the ship reappeared in Norfolk, Virginia, and then back to Philadelphia. It was also seen in 1969 and Lake Mead in 1983.

Nikola Tesla's notes were discovered after he died in 1943 showing he had invented a teleportation device and time machine.

Lawyer Andrew Basiago claimed to be a participant in Project Pegasus, a secret government project that involved experiments with teleportation and both past and future time travel. Andrew is the founder of the Mars Anomaly Research Society (MARS) and the author of the discovery of life on Mars.

While many of us struggle with the complexities of ordinary consciousness, other people naturally can see beyond the limits of time and space. Andrew Basiago became aware of these abilities at a very young age and was tapped for military use. now, he reveals the secret programs that he was once a part of with Project Pegasus in an interview on Audacy.com with Regina Meredith in 2012.

Andrew leads a campaign to lobby the U.S. Government to disclose its secrets on time travel, teleportation, and the U.S. presence on Mars. He served with DARPA (Defense Advanced Research Projects Agency) Project Pegasus at the dawn of the time-space age and was one of humanity.

Basiago also claims that he was transported to Gettysburg, Pennsylvania on the day Abraham Lincoln delivered the Gettysburg Address on November 19, 1863. Andrew Basiago was born in 1961 and was eleven years old in 1971 when he leaped back to the year 1863 for Project Pegasus.

Andrew is the young boy standing in front of the crowd gathered around Lincoln in 1863

Basiago claims the photograph is proof that he time-traveled back to 1863. In this case, he says, he had stepped into a plasma confinement chamber in 1972 and hopped back to 1863 Gettysburg. There, he visited the dedication of the Soldiers' National Cemetery. He also claimed that his original pair of shoes vanished during his voyage in 1863. That's why they appear oversized in the photo. He was given a new pair when he arrived and tried his best to avoid drawing attention to himself. Ultimately, however, he failed, leaving behind a single piece of evidence of his temporal journey—the photograph seen above.

What's most interesting is that this photo is the first ever discovered of Abraham Lincoln at Gettysburg. Josephine Cobb noticed his face while viewing the glass plate negative at the National Archives in 1952. If you zoom in very closely, you can see who historians believe is Lincoln, standing with his hat off in the crowd.

Now, aside from Basiago's story, here's what we know about the photograph. According to the Library of Congress, it was taken at Gettysburg on November 19, 1863, likely by photographer Mathew Brady. It's available in higher quality on the Library of Congress website.

How does time travel affect the present? If Andrew was time traveling in 1972, can you imagine how many others have made the leap into the past and perhaps altered future events, and perhaps not for benevolent reasons?

Have you heard of the Chronovisor, an instrument created in the 1960s, that could see events in the past and even witness historic moments? It was supposed to be a secret, but its existence was leaked to the public. The time machine was created by a group of respected Italian physicists, engineers, and mathematicians led by Pellegrino Ernetti, a Benedictine Friar and former physicist. Ernetti claimed that the machine could look into the past and bring back records of historic events, like a television, using the combination of a cathode-ray tube, dials, antennas, and some sort of resonance amplifier.

The images it supposedly captured from the past appeared in hologram form, and users could rotate them to view different perspectives. The idea behind it is that it was possible to recreate the past through vibrations left in space-time. Essentially, it turned into the frequencies of the past and deconstructed those frequencies into images and sounds, effectively teleporting the user back to that specific moment in time to view.

In the mid-1970s, Father Francois Brune investigated the machine and published a book about it, *The Vatican's New Mystery*. The book described how Father Ernetti witnessed many events like the crucifixion of Christ and the Roman senate meetings. He viewed Napolean Bonaparte's speech to his army, the signing of the Treaty of Westphalia, which ended the Thirty Years War in 1648, and the construction of the Temple of Solomon in Jerusalem.

Was it a hoax or real?

Mark Twain wrote *A Connecticut Yankee in King Arthur's Court* in 1889, a book that explores time travel or time slips, and there's Alison Uttley's novel, *A Traveller in Time,* Marty McFly's troubles in the movie, *Back to the Future,* and the recent time-mangling Netflix series *Dark*. And while intentional time travel is seemingly impossible, there are countless reports of ordinary people who have suddenly experienced a 'time slip'.

Some paranormal investigators speculate that time slips tend to happen in more ancient areas where intense events have occurred.

You're an interesting species. An interesting mix. You're capable of such beautiful dreams, and such horrible nightmares. You feel so lost, so cut off, so alone, only you're not. See, in all our searching, the only thing we've found that makes the emptiness bearable is each other. —From the 1997 movie CONTACT

CHAPTER EIGHTEEN

ORBS, UFOS, AND ETS

In November of 2019 a man in Shreveport, Louisiana was outside when he looked up in the sky to see dozens of orbs and began to video them. He noticed both black and white orbs and how the black ones appeared to be attacking the white orbs. More orbs appeared and then they suddenly vanished. The man believed he was seeing a spiritual war in space between benevolent angels and dark entities.

A video was taken on the afternoon of October 21, 2017, in Long Beach by Jim Martin who was outside mowing his lawn when he spotted a huge white cylindrical object in the sky and three smaller orbs below it. He began talking to the UFOs, "Thank you, brothers." Suddenly the mother ship began releasing smaller orbs that began falling to the ground.

Extraterrestrials are getting us ready for the huge awakening in the next two years! Get your cameras and videos ready!

Will an invasion come from space? Every day there are UFO reports, strange orbs that shapeshift in the sky, and other bizarre sightings worldwide. Reports continue of UFOs dropping small white objects from their spacecraft. I don't want to sound too far out, but what if they are altering human minds with some kind of substance that alters the brain to want violence and anarchy?

I predict a huge event that will appear in the sky in 2024. I'm not sure what it will be, but there will be no doubt that advanced beings exist here.

As I wrote earlier, not all beings visiting Earth or those who live underground and in our deepest oceans are benevolent and spiritual. They want to enslave us.

There's a war taking place between the enslaver Gods and the benevolent spiritual ones. The Dark beings changed the original plans for Earth. They are not evil, but uninformed beings because this is how they believe they must operate. They separated themselves from knowledge as many humans are doing. They hold onto fear and do not honor other life. They use life for their genetic experiments. They are part human and part reptilian.

Don't delude yourself into believing that you have always incarnated as human. You incarnate to experience creation, to gather information about creation, and to comprehend it collectively. Some of you recall another lifetime as an alien living on another planet. If you were just incarnated in one world only, it would be boring. Expand your boundaries and mind and realize that you have to experience many things. There is brilliance within all LIFE.

I have often used the *Star Wars* Cantina scene where Luke Skywalker walks into a bar and sees a variety of aliens as an analogy of the types of beings visiting Earth. Abductees report encounters with insect-like beings (Ant people and Praying Mantis people) and blue Beings, some are human-looking with blonde or red hair—The Nordics, and the Grays have huge heads, large black eyes, and small spindly bodies, and the huge hairy beast called Big Foot lives in wooded areas and seen worldwide might be another alien species.

When humans finally travel the universe they will connect with many creatures, both good and bad, and it will be like Star Wars or Star Trek. The adventure of space travel is in our future.

CHAPTER NINETEEN

2024 PRESIDENTIAL ELECTION

Guess who is behind the curtain in the land of Oz—it's none other than former President Barack Obama pulling the levers for the Biden Administration. Obama helped draft the new 110-page White House Artificial Intelligence Policy that President Joe Biden rolled out the first week of November 2023, according to aides familiar with the situation. The world has seen how quickly AI can evolve—with the potential to change the way we work, learn, and create, but much of this new policy will be aimed at equity and disinformation used against the American people.

President Joe Biden will not be re-elected President in 2024—I guarantee that. He will go down in history books as the worst U.S. President in history for his disastrous withdrawal of all U.S. troops from Afghanistan on August 30,

2021, when thirteen U.S. troops were killed at the Kabul airport by the Taliban, for allowing over 7 million illegal migrants to enter the United States and inundate our major cities, the growing inflation, the failed Green Energy plan, and billions of dollars given to Ukraine, and $14.3 billion pledged to Israel, and possibly $100 million funding to Hamas/Palestine for humanitarian aid to civilians in Gaza and the Israeli-occupied West Bank.

The United States exit from Afghanistan resulted in the Taliban terrorists regaining control of the country and created a refugee crisis as many Afghans fled. Biden didn't go back for as many as 1,500 Americans and those Afghans who aided the United States. Approximately $7 billion worth of U.S. military equipment transferred to the Afghan government over 16 years was left behind allowing the Taliban to confiscate those weapons.

President Biden allowed a Chinese spy balloon to travel across the United States before shooting it down over U.S. territorial waters off the coast of Myrtle Beach, South Carolina, by an aim-9x sidewinder missile fired from a United States Air Force f-22 Raptor that had departed from Langley Air Force base. The balloon traveled across the U.S. from January 28 to February 4, 2023, and originated from China. It flew across North American airspace and bases, including Alaska, and western Canada. Who knows what the Chinese gathered from that balloon before it was shot down?

The Biden Administration doesn't want to offend China even though they are making all the deadly Fentanyl drugs for the Mexican drug cartel who then sell it in the United States. In 2022, 73,654 people, young and old, died from a fentanyl overdose in the United States. By allowing an open border where anyone can make America their home, Biden has made it easy for sex traffickers to kidnap children and sell them.

Trump made sure that America was energy independent, but then Biden stopped oil production in the United States, and now we are dependent on foreign oil. Our military is a joke, and now close to 7 billion illegal migrants—drug cartels, terrorists, sex traffickers of children, have flooded our borders since 2020. None of the migrants have been vaccinated for COVID-19, TB (Tuberculosis), Typhoid, and other diseases eradicated in the United States years ago. Already the Biden administration has given the illegals rooms at expensive hotels in New York City, food, cell phones, and medical treatment while Americans suffer.

Biden loves us so much he calls Trump supporters, "white supremacists," and Hillary Clinton dubbed MAGA Trump supporters as "deplorables," and suggested Trump supporters should be deprogrammed.

Hillary is the one who should have been deprogrammed when she and Bill were involved with MK-Ultra mind control experiments on children and adults. U.S. Central Intelligence Agency (CIA) developed procedures and drugs that could be used during interrogations to weaken people through brainwashing and psychological torture. Read the book, *Trance Formation of America* by Cathy O'Brien and how she was sexually abused by well-known people.

Our oil reserves have been greatly depleted by the Biden Administration. Biden tapped the strategic petroleum reserves last year when Russia's invasion of Ukraine sent oil prices soaring. Republicans blame him for putting the nation's energy security at risk. Biden's administration sold off more than 40 percent of the strategic petroleum reserve in 2022 to help limit rising fuel prices after Russia invaded Ukraine, leaving the stockpile at its lowest levels since the early 1980s.

Countries worldwide don't respect Biden who has shown increased cognitive issues since his election in 2020. Jordan, Egypt, and the Palestinians have canceled meetings 24 hours before he was supposed to meet with them. They've read or heard about Biden's kickbacks from Ukraine's Burisma oil Company with his son Hunter Biden. When Joe Biden became a Senator in 1972, he was not a millionaire, but suddenly he acquired millions of dollars from foreign entities like China, Ukraine, and Romania without owning a business. How is that possible? Biden and his son Hunter have limited liability companies (LLCs) everywhere that the IRS is still investigating.

The United States debt has grown to 33 trillion dollars and rising with Biden's open-pocket spending. The United States would be debt-free if we had oil to sell, but Biden insists we forget about oil and think all electric and "Green Energy."

On November 20, Joe Biden will be 81, and we've seen all his faux pas, how he gets lost on stage, or stumbles and falls. We've seen how he embellishes stories, and how he claims his son Beau died in Iraq, instead of dying from a brain tumor. According to NBC News, Former President Barack Obama quietly advised the White House over the past five months on its strategy to address artificial intelligence, engaging behind the scenes with tech companies and holding Zoom meetings with top West Wing aides at President Joe Biden's request, according to aides to both men.

Biden shows increasing signs of dementia and doctors who have observed him believe his sudden bursts of anger and forgetfulness suggest he's in stage 6 of Alzheimer's Disease. Stage 7 is full-blown Alzheimer's Disease.

The new House Speaker Mike Johnson has started impeachment proceedings on President Biden. If Biden is impeached by the House, it's doubtful it will pass the mostly Democratic Senate and Chuck Schumer will make sure of that.

Joe Biden will not be re-elected President in November of 2024, and the Mideast war will be his Achilles Heel or downfall. Thousands are demonstrating and protesting worldwide against the U.S. involvement in the Israel/Palestine war because of Biden. His poll numbers continue to drop while Trump's polls rise.

Plus, the Biden crime family will finally get their comeuppance in 2024 for their political blackmail of foreign money. More than 40 confidential sources provided "criminal information" related to the Biden family to the FBI – which the Justice Department tried to discredit as "foreign disinformation," according to Republican Sen. Chuck Grassley. The confidential human sources, managed by several different FBI field offices, supplied the bureau with details of potential crimes by Hunter Biden, James Biden, and Joe Biden dating back to his time as vice president, according to a letter, obtained by The Post, that was sent by the Iowa Republican to FBI Director Christopher Wray and Attorney General Merrick Garland on Tuesday. The Biden family had no business being in Ukraine—no personal ties, no business relationships, and no expertise or experience in the energy sector. Yet, Hunter Biden sat on the board of a Ukrainian gas company called Burisma and received millions of dollars in exchange. Subpoenaed bank records show that roughly $20 million in unexplained wire transfers were sent to the Biden family from foreign sources.

The Biden family has been receiving millions of dollars from Ukraine's Burisma and China in exchange for political favors. I believe that those who scream the loudest, have the most to hide. Here's a check that Congress finds suspicious of the Biden and their criminal activities. Why was Joe's brother James paying back $40,000.00 in 2017 before Joe Biden was elected in 2020? According to Republican Congressman James Comer, more evidence is to be presented in the coming months on the Biden family's criminal activities.

SARA AND JAMES BIDEN SR. 6142

Sept 3, 2017 Date

Pay to the Order of Joseph R. Biden, Jr. $40,000.00

Forty-Thousand and 00/100 Dollars

For loan repayment Sara Biden

However, if he is elected again in 2024, it won't be because the election was fair. It will be a rigged election. Already ballot boxes are being tampered with. Many states don't require I.D.s for voting, and that makes it easy for fraud.

Who will be the Democrat nominee in 2024—California's Governor Gavin Newsom, Dean Phillips (representative from Minnesota, Kamala Harris or Michelle Obama?

Recently arrogant California Governor Gavin Newsom met with Chinese Leader Xi Jinping strutting next to the Chinese Leader as if he were already President. He went there to negotiate trade deals between California and the Communist country. I foresee him entering the presidential race even though he has stated he won't. How can you trust someone who won't tell the truth and has ruined California with drugs, homelessness, illegal migrants, and COVID lockdowns that hurt businesses and schools? Gavin Newsom is a Scorpio, the astrological sign of the scorpion. Scorpios can be very manipulative and may twist facts to suit their purpose. Evolved Scorpios are not like this.

Thankfully, there's no way V.P. Kamala Harris will become President.

I will mention this again—for those who believe in all the crazy conspiracy theories circulating on the internet that Biden is a clone and not the real Biden, my question is how could you find someone that inept who can't remember how to get off a stage, can't remember who is wife is, and constantly gives nonsense speeches? As Biden would say, "C'mon, man!"

Consider how House Speaker Kevin McCarthy was ousted out of Congress by eight in Congress led by Republican Congressman Matt Gaetz. Congress became a mess for three weeks without a speaker. On Wednesday, October 25, 2023, Louisiana's Republican Congressman Mike Johnson, a constitutional lawyer, aimed at keeping Donald Trump in power, questioning the legitimacy of the 2020 election. He will be a real plus for Donald Trump in the coming months.

House Speaker Mike Johnson and the Republican-led House passed a resolution declaring solidarity with Israel and pledging to give its government the funding needed to defeat Hamas. Now they've introduced a bill aiming to do just that—but not without controversy. The bill would send $14.3 billion to Israel without addressing funding requests for the war in Ukraine. Johnson's new bill would pay for the spending with $14.5 billion in cuts to the long-understaffed Internal Revenue Service. Biden wants to hire 87,000 new IRS employees. The Bill will either be vetoed by Biden or by the Senate.

Robert F. Kennedy Jr.'s independent bid for president is facing a big hurdle just as it gets off the ground: a grueling, expensive fight to get on the ballot in 50 states and Washington, D.C. He won't go far in 2024 but don't count him out in 2028.

Trump's Fight for 2024

On October 31, 2023, Former President Donald Trump sounded the alarm about the far-left's attempts to remove him from Colorado's 2024 presidential primary ballot.

"A fake trial is currently taking place to try and illegally remove my name from the ballot," Trump said in a Tuesday statement posted to Truth Social. "I often say that 2024 will be the most important election in the history of our country. The reason for that, and that statement, is that our country is being destroyed by people who have no idea what they're doing. Or even worse, they may very well have an idea, they may hate our country, and they may want to see it destroyed.

"But it may also be the last election we ever have. If this election doesn't work, if this election is rigged and stolen, if bad things happen, our country will not survive. If Crooked Joe and the Democrats get away with removing my name from the ballot, then there will never be a free election in America again," Trump continued. "We will have become a dictatorship where your president is chosen for you. You will no longer have a vote, or certainly a meaningful vote. And you could say, frankly, that that has already begun," he said, adding that "this is truly our final chance to save America."

A lawsuit in Colorado is challenging Trump's eligibility for the state's presidential ballot next year, claiming he shouldn't be allowed to run for president because he allegedly violated Section 3 of the 14th Amendment, which prevents someone who "engaged in insurrection or rebellion" from holding federal office.

Article III Project founder and attorney Mike Davis warned on Steve Bannon's "War Room" on Wednesday that "there's no question that Denver District Court Judge Sarah Wallace will disqualify Trump from the Colorado ballot."

"What's going to have to happen is the Supreme Court of the United States that has discretionary review is going to have to put on their big boy pants...they're going to have to take a Trump case because this is so much bigger than President Trump," Davis said. "These are Republic-ending tactics by the left. If you can just take someone off the ballot who's going to win the White House, you're going to take that choice away from the American people based upon a bogus legal theory with activist lawyers and activist judges, we're not going to have a country left."

Before she was appointed a judge, Wallace contributed $100 to the Colorado Turnout Project, a group that was formed in response to the Jan. 6 Capitol protests.

"A contribution to the Colorado Turnout Project shows support for the view that January 6, 2021, constituted an 'insurrection,'" Trump's lawyer Scott Gessler wrote in a filing seeking Wallace's recusal from the case.

Former National Security Adviser Lt. Gen. Mike Flynn likewise warned that the lawsuit raises serious concerns about the future of the country.

"This video below of @realDonaldTrump is a sobering message for ALL Americans," Flynn wrote on X. "Like Trump or not, for him to be speaking like this is a sign of the times we currently face."

Former President Donald Trump is facing two lawsuits to prevent him from being on the ballot in New Hampshire, Colorado, and Minnesota under a rarely-used provision of the 14th Amendment. In Minnesota, the state's Supreme Court is hearing oral arguments Thursday in a lawsuit that was filed by the nonprofit group Free Speech for People, along with former Secretary of State Joan Growe and former Supreme Court Justice Paul H. Anderson.

The lawsuit asks the court to order Democratic Secretary of State Steve Simon to remove Trump from the primary and general election ballot. It mirrors the case in Colorado, arguing that Trump violated his oath of office by stoking an insurrection to overthrow the results of the 2020 election on Jan. 6, 2021, and should therefore be disqualified from holding office again. It has not been proven that he caused an insurrection, yet states are judging him guilty. What kind of justice is this?

Five of the seven state Supreme Court justices are expected to hear the case.

On October 6, 2023, California Governor Gavin Newsom today issued a proclamation calling for a presidential primary election on March 5, 2024. Why would he do that? California has the largest electoral votes in the country, and having early voting there will probably be illegal voting. Seven months before the nationwide Presidential election. He wants to hurt Trump's chances of winning in California.

In October 2023, key figures who sought a share of Trump's reflected glory and status as President turned against him to save themselves by testifying against him for plea deals.

Our country was doing great under Donald Trump's presidency from 2016 to 2020. Gas prices were at $2.49/gallon, we had lots of oil and gas reserves, our Southern and Northern borders were stopping illegals from flooding in, unemployment was low, mortgage rates were at 3% (now nearing 8%) and people had great 401k plans. So why did the American Citizens vote for Biden? Wouldn't it make more sense to vote for someone who has made great strides in Making America Great? Even our enemies respected Donald Trump, and they don't respect Joe Biden.

Will Trump go to prison...NO! From everything I've read on the internet even if Trump is convicted of a felony, he can still run for President of the United States. 2023 has been a tough year for him and it won't get easier into 2024. Already the Judges and District Attorney's charging him have made it impossible for him to campaign each month without having to appear in different courts. It's insane. If Trump dropped out as a candidate for President, charges would probably be dropped or reduced, but I don't foresee him dropping out.

I've predicted the Democratic Left will go to any length to stop him from becoming President in 2024. Even former Fox host Tucker Carlson suggested the Left might try to assassinate him. Again, I don't foresee this happening.

However, the odds are mounting against him, yet Trump has always bounced back, and proven that he was not involved in any Russian collusion as the FBI, the Democratic Left, and the Biden Administration accused him of. 2024 is a number one year for him which means new beginnings.

Here's the good news. A recent poll taken shows President Biden is trailing Donald J. Trump in five of the six most important battleground states one year before the 2024 election, suffering from enormous doubts about his age and deep dissatisfaction over his handling of the economy and a host of other issues, new polls by The New York Times and Siena College have found.

The results show Mr. Biden losing to Mr. Trump, his likeliest Republican rival, by margins of three to 10 percentage points among registered voters in Arizona, Georgia, Michigan, Nevada, and Pennsylvania. Mr. Biden is ahead only in Wisconsin, by two percentage points, the poll found. Across the six battlegrounds—all of which Mr. Biden carried in 2020 the president trails by an average of 48 to 44 percent.

Discontent pulsates throughout the Times/Siena poll, with a majority of voters saying Mr. Biden's policies have personally hurt them. The survey also reveals the extent to which the multiracial and multigenerational coalition that elected Mr. Biden is fraying. Demographic groups that backed Mr. Biden by landslide margins in 2020 are now far more closely contested, as two-thirds of the electorate sees the country moving in the wrong direction.

Trump supporters may not like his bombastic rhetoric, but they do like the way he gets things done. Still, there are those die-hard Democrats who only listen to the fake news and have no idea how much Trump accomplished in four short years as president. Trump will still have the major issues to overcome like the classified documents stored at his Mar-a-Lago home in Florida. We still don't know why Biden could store classified documents during his Vice President years at his Delaware home garage and other places without any consequence. Yes, the Republicans held hearings on Biden's classified documents, but no further action has been taken. We don't even know what was in those documents for Trump or Biden.

October 19, 2023, former Donald Trump campaign lawyer Sidney Powell's stunning plea deal in the Georgia election subversion case on the eve of her trial will significantly change the landscape of the ongoing state and federal prosecutions against former president Trump. Powell was still posting claims on social media that said the 2020 election was rigged against Trump, yet on Thursday, she walked into an Atlanta courtroom and admitted that she was guilty of trying to interfere with the 2020 election. Justice Department Special Counsel Jack Smith, who filed federal election subversion charges against Trump, might now get a bunch of new evidence, thanks to Powell.

Whatever statements or testimony she provides to Georgia State prosecutors, and federal investigators will try to use it against Trump in his Federal trial scheduled to begin in March 2024, in Washington, D.C. Furthermore, Powell was an unindicted co-conspirator in Trump's federal indictment, suggesting that the special counsel believes she broke the law. This puts her in danger of potential Federal charges, so she may seek to cooperate with Smith as well.

Trump is now in the last year of his current nine-year cycle in 2023 which means endings, transitions, and people leaving his life with the status quo upset. If he was operating in his life in harmony with the universal energies, he would have gained much experience and knowledge over the past nine years and would be re-elected. There is also the opposite if his life has been out of balance, he will experience loss, heartache, and upheaval in the final months of 2024. The full tapes of January 6, 2020, are to be released soon and the truth will be shown. Why were many Trump supporters imprisoned when Hamas supporters also entered the Capitol building recently? It's called lop-sided justice.

During a rally in Iowa, former President Trump told supporters that he was willing to go to jail for the country. He'd never go to prison and how would the justices allow the Secret Service into prison to guard him? They couldn't. Again,

I don't foresee him serving a prison sentence.

Trump faces 91 felony counts in four criminal cases in Washington, D.C., New York, Florida, and Georgia. Trump has been mistreated by corrupt President Biden, the DOJ, District Attorneys, and the rest of the Democrats because they want to stop him from being elected in 2024. They will go to any length to stop him.

Could a president serve from prison? That's less clear. The newest criminal counts against Trump include conspiracy to defraud the United States; conspiracy to obstruct an official proceeding; obstruction of and attempt to obstruct an official proceeding; and conspiracy against rights.

Those are in addition to a total of 40 counts in a separate federal indictment related to the special counsel's investigation into the mishandling of classified documents, as well as 34 felony criminal charges of falsifying business records in Manhattan related to an alleged hush money payment scheme and cover-up involving an adult film star.

If Trump were to be convicted before the 2024 election and win the nomination for President, he could try to grant himself a pardon, according to various sources. "The Constitution has very few requirements to serve as President, such as being at least 35 years of age. It does not bar anyone indicted or convicted, or even serving jail time, from running as president and winning the presidency.

If Trump is convicted as a felon, he will never be able to leave the United States like all convicted felons.

I predict that Trump will win the election in 2024, but there's a caveat to it and that depends on election integrity and what happens with his indictments. However, each time the Democratic Left indicts him his poll numbers rise. Even when a judge threatens to imprison him for speaking out, his poll numbers rise.

Events are still forming and all of you reading this, please pray for Trump, and I mean pray. Kneel before God and pray with all your heart and soul. A civil war is still looming in the future.

America's future and the world's freedom is at stake now. Marxism is taking over and if the Democrats win in 2024, you might feel as if you were put in a concentration camp.

There are those dark individuals who believe that MAGA supporters and Christians are the real terrorist threat in the United States. But they are a threat to our freedom and our democracy. That's evil and bigoted thinking.

The Psychic Twins on Trump

The renowned Psychic Twins, Linda and Terry Jamison are identical twins based in Los Angeles, California who claim to be accurate psychics. The Jamisons' predictions have been featured in tabloid newspapers, and they have appeared in various media.

"On August 14th, an Atlanta Grand Jury indicted Trump and 18 others on charges for a wide-ranging illegal Rico scheme to overturn the former president's 2020 electoral defeat. All the conspirators surrendered and were arrested in the Fulton County jail in Atlanta. Trump is seen looking defiant in his infamous mug shot, the first time for a former president.

"The historic indictment is the fourth criminal case Trump has been charged within the last few months. The charges follow a sweeping investigation by Fulton County District Attorney Fani Willis of the efforts by Trump and his allies to reverse the 2020 presidential election results. Unlike the election subversion charges brought by Special Counsel Jack Smith, Trump will not be able to pardon himself if reelected in 2024. We do not believe that Trump will win the presidential election in 2024."

The Stars Speak

Trump was born under the star Capella, located in the Alpha Aurigae Constellation. The star imparts honor and prominent positions of trust as well as wealth and success. But he must learn to listen to others to avoid misunderstanding. He can be trustworthy, inquisitive, and also argumentative, and indecisive. We've seen how bombastic and animated he can be, and prone to embellishing facts.

Trump should have won in 2020, and if it wasn't by ballot fraud, it was by Twitter and Facebook censoring people who tried to post stories about Hunter Biden's corruption with Burisma in Ukraine. This was voter tampering by censorship even if there isn't proof of machine ballot fraud.

Trump made these great changes to America from 2016 and 2020:

Trump made the United States the number one producer of oil and natural gas in the world. We were energy-independent.

He kept our borders safer, although some migrants still crossed, but not the millions crossing since President Biden took office in 2021 and opened the gates to the U.S. for millions of illegal migrants from countries worldwide.

The Tax Cuts and Jobs Act expanded School Choice, allowing parents to use up to $10,000 from a 529 education savings account to cover K-12 tuition costs at the public, private, or religious school of their choice.

Trump launched a new pro-American lesson plan for students called *The 1776 Commission* to promote patriotic education. Prohibited the teaching of Critical Race Theory in the Federal government.

Signed into law *The Strengthening Career and Technical Education* for the 21st Century Act, which provides over 13 million students with high-quality vocational education and extends more than $1.3 billion each year to states for critical workforce development programs.

Signed the INSPIRE Act which encouraged NASA to have more women and girls participate in STEM and seek careers in aerospace.

The DOJ charged more than 65 defendants collectively responsible for distributing over 45 million opioid pills. Brought kingpin designations against traffickers operating in China, India, Mexico, and more who have played a role in the epidemic in America.

Indicted major Chinese drug traffickers for distributing fentanyl in the U.S. for the first time, and convinced China to enact strict regulations to control the production and sale of fentanyl.

Rebuilt the military and created the Sixth Branch, the United States Space Force. Completely rebuilt the United States military with over $2.2 trillion in defense spending, including $738 billion for 2020.

Secured three pay raises for our service members and their families, including the largest raise in a decade.

Established the Space Force, the first new branch of the United States Armed Forces since 1947.

With all the pork barrel spending on idiotic pet projects by Congress in their 500-page bill, we could see a government shutdown on November 17, 2023.

'Pork barrel' is a term used in politics and refers to national government politicians spending huge amounts of money in their local voting districts to encourage voters to re-elect them at the next election. The idea behind the practice is that the money allocated to the representative's district will benefit the lives of the local constituents, thereby securing their support and votes. Support in this context can also mean contributions to that politician's next election campaign.

At a time when Americans continue to suffer from the highest inflation in 40 years, members of Congress increased the cost earmarks by 38.1 percent or more than seven times the 5 percent rate of inflation. Congress gets the bacon, and we get greased!

The United States' debt stands at 33 trillion dollars. The $33 trillion is gross federal debt that includes debt held by the public as well as debt held by Federal Trust Funds and other Government accounts. In very basic terms, this can be thought of as debt that the government owes to others plus the debt it owes to itself.

Biden won't stop his spending on war for Ukraine and now Israel. The Biden Administration and Congress have directed more than $75 billion in assistance to Ukraine, which supposedly includes humanitarian, financial, and military support. So far there's been no accountability for the use of that money.

On October 4, 2023, owner of the Skinwalker Ranch Brandon Fugal discussed the 2024 *Secret of Skinwalker Ranch,* Season 5 on his website. He mentioned former House Speaker Nancy Pelosi as corrupt from the millions of dollars she's made in Congress from insider trading. She's not the only one who has reaped huge amounts of money while in Congress and the Senate through political favors and insider trading, and became millionaires. Pelosi will be indicted for her insider trading and may several some time in jail.

Poor Martha Stewart spent five months in minimum security at Alderson Federal Prison Camp in West Virgins in 2004 and was released in March 2005 for insider trading, a felony, but you'll never see Nancy Pelosi in jail for insider trading. The Democrats can get away with everything and never get charged or indicted, but if the Republicans tried that, they'd be in prison for life.

Republican Candidates

So far Trump is the favorite Republican candidate, and he's far ahead of Biden and all the other Republican candidates, yet he comes with a lot of baggage and won't be able to campaign as he planned into 2024. Mike Pence recently dropped out. Iowa Governor Kim Reynold recently endorsed Ron DeSantis for President. If Trump is re-elected, he would only have four short years to drain the swamp in Washington, D.C., remove over 7 million illegal migrants, restore our energy reserves, bring back gas drilling again, stop a civil war in America, stop World War III, reverse inflation, put a halt on electric cars, and stop the unvetted illegals migrants from the continued nonstop flow into the United States from countries worldwide that include terrorists.

If only we could have had Trump for eight years straight years our country would not be in the mess it is in today.

The free will of the people will shape the future in 2024.

In 2016, it was six months before Trump was elected, I had a powerful vision of him taking the oath of President on a cloudy day with a dark overcoat and Melania wearing a light-colored coat. It turned out to be true. Trump wore a black overcoat and Melania wore a light blue coat. The vision was like watching television—it was so clear. My prediction was carried on NewsMax before the election: **https://www.newsmax.com/Headline/Psychics-divided-Election/2016/11/05/id/757228/**

Anything can happen between now and next year. Will Trump stay healthy even though he's going through a tumultuous time in his life and extreme stress? He's not in the best of physical shape at age seventy-seven, and stress could certainly affect his health. But I believe he is destined to be re-elected. Although I felt he would be re-elected in 2020, I didn't foresee voter ballot fraud taking place.

In my last book, *Prophecy Now*, I predicted Governor Ron Ron DeSantis could be our next president. If something happens to Trump, Ron DeSantis would be next in line. I don't foresee any of the other candidates continuing—Tim Scott, Vivek Ramaswamy, Chris Christie, or Nikki Haley.

I thought I'd add this about Ron DeSantis. I listened to an astrologer who said Ron DeSantis doesn't have anything special in his astrological chart except his moon is in Aquarius and on July 4, 1776, at 4:50 p.m. Eastern time, our founding Fathers issued the Declaration of Independence by the Continental Congress, severing our political connections to Great Britain. On that date, the Moon was Aquarius. DeSantis is connected to our country with his Moon in Aquarius.

However, DeSantis is a Virgo, and Virgos are not the easiest people to know or understand. They are perfectionists and they demand that from the people who work for them. I predicted that he would enter the race for President by the first of the year. He registered to run for President of the United States on May 24, 2023.

Florida Governor Ron DeSantis will be forty-six in 2024. His primary star is Denebola, found in the Constellation Beta Leo. His astrology shows that he will have exciting events and opportunities in his life. But the benefits may not be long-lasting, and it warns about watching his temper or being anxious which can spoil relationships. The star bestows good judgment, daring, courage, and a generous nature. This star warns against hasty decisions.

DeSantis won't be president in 2024 unless something unforeseen happens to Trump. But look for him to return in 2028.

Unlike Donald Trump who made some risqué remarks about women, and was known to cheat on his wife Melania, DeSantis is known as a good husband and a father, and an excellent governor to Florida. He kept Florida's business going during the COVID pandemic and didn't force Florida citizens to take the COVID-19 vaccine or wear masks. He even allowed his Florida citizens to try monoclonal treatments at clinics. During the destructive hurricane Ian that hit Florida in late September 2022, he had volunteers and first responders on the scene helping victims. He stopped woke companies like Disney from pushing their agenda in Florida, and he banned CRT (critical race theory) in schools. He's and mover and shaker in politics and "a straight shooter."

I find it interesting that both Trump and DeSantis were born on the 14th day of the month. People traits of people born on the 14th day of the month include confidence, determination, leadership, creativity, resourcefulness, charisma, a connection to the spiritual world, and previous lives. They have a karmic connection!

CHAPTER TWENTY

MORE PREDICTIONS

Have you tried to see a specialist doctor or a family physician and found out they are booked for months? It's going to get increasingly worse as the millions of illegal migrants need surgery, and treatment for diseases, Pregnancy, and other major health issues.

President Biden will make sure they get help before you do. The migrant surge is overwhelming border towns and hospitals.

Some of these predictions as interpretations of Nostradamus's prophecies:

- Bloodshed and plagues. A war to end all wars with the East against the West.
- Lightning to nations. Terror from the sky.
- People blaspheme against God.

- Slaughter through the City. Site of Armageddon.
- The mightiest earthquake shakes islands, and mountains fall. Beware Rome.
- Torrential storms, whirlwind from the North. False miracles abound. Earth out of course.
- A third day of darkness.
- The Royal Palace assailed by fire in the sky.
- An entire people silent, and afraid to tell the truth.
- Fire from heaven, Loyal City consumed.
- A sudden scourge. Darkness at noon. Third day of the month. Mist, gloom, famine, and fear. Vermillion Sun, hidden moon. A stench in the air as celestial armies arrive.
- Ingenious conspiracy.
- Rebellion subdued by the Rod of Iron, over sky, sea, and snow.
- The Great Comforter pacifies Earth. The Golden Millennium.

Betsey's Predictions for the Future

- A Middle East country will carry out biological weapons attacks in the escalating war between Israel and Palestine.
- Crime will escalate in major cities, citizens will need to carry guns to protect themselves.
- Stay aware if you live in big cities of bomb attacks. Stay away from large gatherings anywhere in the United States, France, and the UK.
- NASA will launch the Artemis Mission in the next two years landing the first woman and first person of color on the moon, using innovative technologies to explore more of the lunar surface than ever before. They might be stopped by beings that live inside the hollow moon.
- Commercial airlines hijacked.
- As I predicted in my past prophecy books including *Prophecy Now,* COVID-19 will be endemic like the flu or the common cold.

- Robots will become more and more useful and more intelligent—frighteningly so.
- Musk's first manned mission to Mars will happen within five years.
- Space war with satellites.
- Gas and oil rates increase as the Mideastern war continues into 2024. Oil depletion in the United States from Biden giving Ukraine more oil reserves.
- Border Agents at war with cartels. Blood on the border as cartels use bombs.
- More financial and legal problems for Trump in 2024. More gag orders to stop him from talking about his court cases and more fines that might lead to jail time. Former employees jumping ship and testifying against him. Even if he is jailed for speaking out by a judge, his poll number will continue to climb. In reality, the more they try to hurt Trump, the more he will rise in popularity. As long as there is no voter tampering in 2024, he will return as President in 2024.
- AI will be used to create deepfakes. AI-generated images are more realistic and more available than ever. What is real and what is fake? It will be impossible to tell.
- Banks closing in record numbers and major stores.
- Fresh vegetables and fruit will be hard to find. Scarcities at grocery stores in 2024.
- Bankruptcies and home foreclosures climb in 2024.
- Inflation growing, and people are unable to afford climbing prices everywhere.
- Space wars and the use of satellites for war.
- Waters poisoned—unclear where, but hundreds die.
- United States ammunition is low and there is a world shortage.
- More mass killings will take place, but not by the insane or mentally ill, but by mind-controlled subjects. Watch how the news will be used to divert your attention from one breaking news to another news event.
- Pro-Palestinian rallies held in the U.S. and worldwide

will turn more violent.

- U.S. Military and ships are scattered worldwide in conflicts. Sitting ducks for China, Iran, and Russia.
- The U.S. Military will reinstitute the draft.
- Airlines strike, truck drivers, and strikes in Hollywood.
- Electric cars will sit on lots unsold. Auto manufacturers furious with Biden's push to sell them.
- A huge solar flare knocks out the power grid for days. Geomagnetic flares will cause powerful earthquakes and volcanic eruptions worldwide.
- An alteration in the orbit of the Earth. The orbits of bodies in the solar system are determined by gravitational forces and are always prone to change. Such an event would have dramatic outcomes for Earth such as climate disruption, spiking radiation levels, and all-round chaos.
- GMOs aka bioengineered food added to everything we eat. Most already have it.
- Humans will be 'tweaked' on a genetic level—eyes, ancestry, build, intelligence. Sometime in the future babies will be grown in tubes, also used in alien technology.
- Weather is out of control worldwide again with flash floods, continued wildfires, huge waves inundating coasts, Category 5 Hurricanes like the one that hit Acapulco, Mexico in October 2023, and stronger tornadoes that last longer. Huge snowstorms and frigid temperatures throughout Europe and part of the Midwest and Eastern U.S.
- Breakthroughs in medicine and eventually a cancer cure. Medications for chronic diseases of the nervous system. The blind will eventually see, but not through their eyes, but in their brains. Something will be attached to the head and will allow limited eyesight.
- Mike Johnson of Louisiana was elected Speaker of the House on October 25, 2023. He is ultra-conservative and pro-life and that will upset the Left.
- Mass protests worldwide become violent against

Israel and Jews everywhere. Jews attacked. Death worldwide!

- Universities without donations due to pro-Palestine rallies and violent rhetoric against the Jews. Students without jobs in the future.
- Civil War in the United States and other countries including China and Iran.
- World War III could begin anytime as the war escalates and spreads in the Mideast. Iran and Lebanon fired on U.S. military stationed in the region.
- Donald Trump will make a startling statement in the coming months.
- Already some websites are being censored on Google and YouTube. Censorship will worsen as November 2024 nears.
- China will attack Taiwan and North Korea will attack South Korea as world wars heat up.
- A nuclear bomb explodes—millions dead.
- UFOs everywhere, thousands of them over major cities. It will look like an invasion, but it won't be.
- Major earthquake shakes the Vatican.
- Strange sightings in the sky. People on their knees in prayer asking for forgiveness.
- America's debt continues to climb, spending by Biden and Democrats. Bankruptcy nears if oil is not produced in America.
- Less freedom for Europeans. Flights canceled due to terrorist threats.
- Biden impeached, but not passed by the Senate. FBI continues to protect Hunter Biden from prosecution as well as the rest of the Biden crime family. Investigations continue by Congress.
- Major discoveries in Egypt—an underground chamber filled with texts. The earliest human relative found possessed metal tools.
- Megathrust earthquake in the South Pacific, huge tsunamis, and volcanoes erupting.
- Prince Harry, Duke of Sussex, and Meghan Markle,

Duchess of Sussex, will divorce in 2024 or 2025. Their marriage has been on the rocks for a long time. Harry will return to the United Kingdom.

- If Donald Trump is elected, he will send most of the illegal migrants back to their countries of origin. He promised that in recent rally speeches.
- Pope Francis will either step down as Pope in 2024 or pass away from respiratory illness.
- The global depopulationists are unleashing a new 'plandemic' to scare the public into submitting to a global UN treaty that controls all bodies on Earth. This could disrupt the 2024 election. Another shutdown—it's possible!
- Coal plants to be shut down in the U.S. More control for the Family of Dark against humanity. They will control our energy, food, and money if they aren't stopped.
- A new illness hits China and children worldwide. Pneumonia that won't react to antibiotics.
- The gap between the elite wealthy and the middle class will become greater. There will be those that have, and who are greedy, and care less about the masses. There will be masses starving. There will be much dissension and conflict worldwide.

CHAPTER TWENTY-ONE

LAURA ABOLI

People are awakening to the dark agenda for humanity. One such person is UK's Laura Aboli. She wrote this on her website: "I have always been a very private person, never particularly active on social media or public platforms. Very much a hermit, I am happiest at home with my kids. But recently I felt the urge to speak my mind, not just privately (which I have always done) but publicly. I suddenly felt compelled to come out of my comfort zone and share my thoughts, opinions, and experience in the hope that I may inspire and encourage a positive change in society. I took a leap of faith that I could make a difference, at least I would try. I am a firm believer that each and everyone can make a difference, and in that spirit, I started writing my blog and making videos with the underlying aim to remind us all of the beauty, power, and resilience of the human spirit."

Laura is the founder of UDIMAF (United Democratic International Movement for Awareness and Freedom) since May 2020. Its goal is to inspire and assist change in society as a direct response to the way events surrounding the global pandemic were affecting people's livelihoods, mental health, and behavior. As a successful entrepreneur with a background in intelligence and information gathering, Laura felt the urge to do something to counteract the fear and the mind control that was leading people to willingly accept the unacceptable: the loss of freedom, the restriction of civil rights, and the imposition of a 'new normality' based on separation, alienation, disconnection, and total control.

Laura's incredible speech can be heard on social media https://www.facebook.com/reel/169102299563397

The final goal is to eradicate. Once you understand the final destination it becomes much easier to look back and identify the psychological conditioning, the biological tampering, the cultural grooming, and the educational prepping that we have been subjected to for decades in preparation to make us accept a posthuman future.

It takes a lot of physical and psychological abuse to get an intelligent species like ours to agree to its own extinction. Most, if not all that has transcended in the last 60 years was designed to get us closer to accepting such a dystopian reality. Whether you care to accept it or not, we live in a hyper-controlled matrix where our perception of reality is meticulously planned, managed, and executed in order to control and steer us in whichever direction they wish. And the direction is a post-human world.

For this, they first needed to destabilize, dehumanize, and demoralize humanity through every means possible. The destruction of the nuclear family, children being indoctrinated by the state, abortion, the eradication of God and spirituality from education, life in megacities, and away from nature, toxic food, air, and water, social media replacing real human connection and interaction, engineered financial crisis and taxation, endless wars and massive migration, stress, anxiety, depression, drugs, and alcohol, constant fearmongering, moral relativism as the new religion. And I could go on and on about how humanity has been influenced and forced to move away from all the things that give us strength, security, purpose, and meaning.

A weak, immoral, disconnected, ignorant, and unhealthy population is an easy target for the next stage—the creation of an entire generation of androgynous beings. Masculinity is under attack psychologically, culturally, and biologically. Women are being replaced in sports, entertainment, and politics by men pretending to be women, and children are being indoctrinated at school to think that gender is a choice.

The transgender movement is not a grassroots movement. It comes from the top. It has nothing to do with people's freedom of expression, sexuality, or civil rights. It is an evil psy-op with a clear agenda to get us closer to transhumanism by making us question the most fundamental notion of human identity—our gender.

If you don't know who you are, if you already identify as a hybrid between a man and a woman, you will be easily convinced to become a hybrid between human and machine.

Gender ideology is the two plus two equals five from George Orwell's *1984* dystopian novel. It's the final test to see if we will follow the most absurd party line towards our own extinction. But two plus two equals four and no matter how you choose to dress, call yourself, or change your physique will not change that. The sad reality though is that in the gaslighting process, we grow closer to a posthuman future. They have mentally and physically harmed an increasing number of children and young people. And it's only getting worse. This must be stopped!

Betsey's comment:
Are we moving toward what abductees have experienced with gray aliens and how they look identical—androgynous, have no emotions, and seem robotic? Perhaps this is our dystopian future if we don't change now.

A generation that hates war will not bring peace. A generation that loves peace will bring peace. — Seth channeled by Jane Roberts

AFTERWORD

2024 will be a karmic year totaling the number 8. Number 8 is important as it represents balance in the spiritual and materialistic world, with Saturn as the ruling planet. 2024 will be an unpredictable year. Events will appear to go one way, and then suddenly change. It will be a flip-flop year of events.

A great number have been mind-controlled into believing whatever the Family of Dark spews from their lips. Together, we have allowed this evil to descend on Earth, individually and collectively. They know how easily manipulated humanity is from our history. Every reactive scenario has been dissected to the cellular level and with restrictive actions planned for each of us.

One thing humanity must learn is that the gravitational field does not hold us here. It is consciousness! The Family of Dark knows that their thoughts can influence the outcome of the experiment. Now the challenge comes to those who desire to be the instruments of changing the negative plans for the destiny of this planet. Can each of you expand your consciousness to encompass the process that lies just beyond your grasp? To leave the known and desire to venture into the unknown requires the courage to release what you feel is the advancement this "civilization" has made from its Stone Age beginnings into modern technological comfort for many on this planet. Did you know that the word civilization is synonymous with slavery?

How does humanity transcend this habitual activity when it is deeply engrained at a planetary level? It has now reached a point where humans cannot break this addiction. Our adversaries know this well. They are sure that humanity cannot change. So how will the shift to a new paradigm of experience start?

It can be done by understanding that thought-focused and released can indeed act within itself and upon itself. Though it sounds simplistic, and it is in reality, it is a powerful tool. For this process to work, some criteria must be present. The intent of its purpose is the key to its success and coordination with and within the flow of Divine Order. Purity of intent to harmonize as the motive is a primary prerequisite.

The outlining thought must be specific only in the intent of purpose. You must visualize another outcome as if you were watching a movie. How do you want the play to end—in a positive or negative way? You must provide direction of purpose allowing the thought thinking process to proceed into Divine Order by releasing it in total trust knowing it will then manifest into this recognizable reality using all the available triggers for appropriate interaction. This is not a plan conceived at a moment's notice. It has been planned over eons of time. Prime events have controlled us in modern times—Wars, JFK assassination, 9-11, COVID-19, and now the Israeli-Hamas war. Courtney Brown, a remote viewer asked his other remote viewers to look at the October 7 where Hamas slaughtered innocent Israeli citizens, and they all said it was allowed to happen to start a war. This is how Wars are started.

Remember, the Bible says that God created nothingness into solid material with his words and thoughts. If we don't awaken to how powerful thoughts are, the intent is that our reality of this earthly experience will continue a pattern of downward movement into the darker and heavier energies that are at the lower end of the scale in which the human body can exist.

Why was this allowed to continue? The freewill aspect is what has been exploited as the basis for their ability to manipulate humanity to be a vehicle of their power. Ours is the exact state of consciousness to serve their purpose. Humans are malleable enough to be influenced into desiring change when pressure is applied to the Soul/extension connection, and change is exactly what they want. Think about how most of you were pressured to get the disastrous COVID-19 vaccine that has caused horrific side effects in great numbers and also killed people. You bought into their fear and did it without trusting your own inner voice and intuition that told you not to get the vaccine.

There is a point at which their restrictive pressure of controlling the mass consciousness of the planet can backfire and cause the exact opposite of what they have planned. This will cause them to miss the opportunity for the final dimensional vibratory change needed for the completion of their plans. It's time to show the Family of Dark how powerful The Family of Light can be by altering their heinous plans for us.

Our world turned upside down in three short years—and it wasn't from a geological event, not yet anyway. Terrorists became heroes, criminals, and murderers became good guys and released from prison, and victims became criminals convicted as such. Words were changed, books banned, people censored, and historical statues removed as if the past could be erased by their removal. Young people became mind-controlled on social media and in schools and colleges, they became indoctrinated in Marxism, critical race theory, hate and bigotry, antisemitism, and transgenderism. People protesting worldwide for the genocide of the Jews, human beings like all of us because they are being seduced by satanic leaders. Drugs flow freely in cities where mindless zombies sway back and forth, unable to stand upright. Their mindlessness lowers the vibrational rate in each city.

To change events unfolding and alter the future, it takes mass consciousness to go into action for the most benevolent outcome. If humans seek genocide of the Jewish nation, how can there ever be peace on Earth? Earth is a stage and we are the actors writing the lines of the script, but until we can figure out the point of the script, there is none! The focused group, The Family of Dark are the ones who have figured it out but their intent is not in harmony with the Creator of the stage and the theatre that this play is being performed upon. They intend to destroy the audience, the actors, the state, and the theatre.

Nothing that we have done in the past has changed anything, so we must become creative and use our brains to get out of this mess of a world. We must depend on ourselves to devise nonviolent ways to nullify the Family of Dark's plans for us and Earth. We must make a Cosmic leap to a level of creative discussion in groups. Our ancestors were clever and used codes to communicate.

"Where two or more of you are gathered together in my Name, there am I also," it says in the Bible. Jesus said, "Truly I tell you, if you have faith as small as a mustard seed, you can say to this mountain, 'move from here to there,' and it will move. nothing will be impossible for you." Matthew 17:20-21.

Humans are powerful together. It just takes faith and belief.

Every day humans receive doses of thought control where the media repeats the news to their slanted agenda. It's as if the pandemic and COVID-19 vaccines altered human brains preventing critical thinking. No one seems to think anymore. It's all about emotions and what I call the "monkey see, monkey do reactions." The saying refers to the act of imitation, usually with limited knowledge and/or concern for the consequences.

You aren't cool if you don't protest against the system.

People have become programmed robots through repeated mind control by teachers, college professors, the news media, politicians, and our leaders. Critical thinking no longer exists.

Instead of the young changing our world with medicine, astronomy, and science, they spend their time on the Chinese-owned TikTok posting stupid, narcissistic videos. But it's not only young people spending their time on Facebook, Twitter, Instagram, and TikTok. Adults are easily influenced too. Women more so.

Some people spend their whole day posting anything they see on YouTube and other channels. What a waste of time and energy when nothing creative is taking place. I'd rather see these people get away from the mind-controlled internet and explore nature and interact more with others on a personal level. Humans have lost touch with each other. We no longer call our friends or family but instead text them or message them on Facebook. What a sad way to live!

As my Great Aunt Grace often said, "The world is going to hell in a handbasket." If she were alive today, she'd be appalled at how people have become Socialists and Marxists since her generation feared Communism would take over the world. If any of the people now radicalized could spend time in Gaza, China, North Korea, Iran, and other tyrannical countries, they would forever love America and what it stands for. Recently, pro-Hamas/Palestine protestors in the United States have called for the destruction of America and the genocide of the Jewish people. A large number of protestors are in the United States on Visas to attend universities and colleges, but why are they in the U.S.? You'd think they'd return to their home countries to defend them. It's easy to speak boldly in safe surroundings. Would they speak so courageously if they were placed in the Mideast war?

Yesterday, November 4, 2023, thousands of angry Hamas/Palestine supporters/protestors marched on Washington, D.C. A great number of these people aren't even from the Mideast, and they have no idea what they are doing. They get their news from Chinese-controlled TikTok.

Dr. Brian Weiss has written many books on reincarnation and the stories of people who were regressed through hypnosis and recalled past lives. Every soul on this Earth has worn different shoes in different times and places, in both male and female bodies, and lived lives as black, white, yellow, red, and brown-skinned people. You might have been a Roman soldier, a slave, a murderer, a pauper in rags, a monk, a nun, or a vicious ruler. If the world believed in reincarnation, they'd think twice about harming God's creations.

In Weiss's book, *Through Time into Healing*, he writes that in Judaism, a fundamental belief in reincarnation, or *gilgul,* has existed for thousands of years. This belief had been a basic cornerstone of the Jewish faith until approximately 1800-1850 when the urge to "modernize" and to be accepted by more scientific communities. However, the belief in reincarnation had been fundamental and mainstream until this time, less than two centuries ago. In orthodox and Chasidic communities, belief in reincarnation continues unabated today. The Kabbala, mystical Jewish literature dating back thousands of years, is filled with references to reincarnation. Rabbi Moshe Chaim Luzzatto, one of the most brilliant Jewish scholars of the past several centuries, summed up gilgul (cycle) in his book, *The Way of God*: "A single soul can be reincarnated several times in different bodies, and in this manner, it can rectify the damage in previous incarnations. Similarly, it can also attain perfection that was not attained in its previous incarnations."

Weiss goes on to write that the history of Christianity contains early references to reincarnation in the New Testament but was deleted in the fourth century by Emperor Constantine when Christianity became the official religion of the Roman Empire. The emperor felt that the concept of reincarnation was threatening to the stability of the empire. Citizens who believed that they would have another chance to live might be less obedient and law-abiding than those who believed in a single Judgment Day for all.

As late as the twelfth century, the Christian Cathars of Italy and southern France were severely brutalized for their belief in reincarnation. People were brutally punished for unorthodox beliefs, the groups learned to keep them secret. The repressions of past life teachings have been political, not spiritual.

If every soul on planet Earth believed in the doctrine of reincarnation and knew that if they harmed or killed a woman, man, or child in the present life, they'd meet a similar fate in a future lifetime. Reincarnation and karma are the laws of the Universe, and no one can escape them. You reap what you sow. But that rule can be altered. Some are not punishments from a past life, or even lessons or patterns carried forward from past lives. By choosing to come into a particular family or constellation of circumstances you have not agreed to submit to abuse. However, you did agree to participate in a certain lesson or type of drama. You still have free will on how a particular lesson or teaching is carried out and so do the other individuals who have chosen to share the lifetime with you. Part of the learning process is learning not to choose the more harmful or destructive paths. Growth can occur easily and joyfully as well as through struggle, and there are many gradations between the two.

The potential for abuse will exist, but it is not inevitable.

But when you die, you will have a full life review of all the things you did and thought, both good and bad, including the hurt and harm done to others. Everything in life is recorded on the Cosmic Computer. There is no way of avoiding the life review.

My mother recalled a past life as a Chinese laborer who worked on the Great Wall of China, and through the years family members have returned in spirit to prove life goes on. The soul never dies. We are endless beings given the spark of life by a magnificent Creator.

As I have written before in prophecy books, we are the Atlanteans who lived when Atlantis was a civilization that reached the pinnacles of sciences and technology, yet this misused their powers. What is happening in the world today, has happened before, but we have not learned our lesson about honoring Earth and all creation, and until we get it, there will be no peace on Earth.

We are also truth seekers and as we seek the truth our bubble of innocence will burst, and we will find ourselves on the ground, bruised from the fall but stronger and wiser. The distressing, disturbing, and disruptive experiences that will come our way may be there for us to heal them and not for us to feel wounded by them. The wealth of *Galactic Knowing* will encompass a healing far vaster than we can imagine. We must become one with all Life. Turn on your emotions now and begin to feel again.

Changes will occur like a pebble skipping across an ocean, as small pebbles turn into huge waves worldwide. Remember in the Bible that little David put a rock into a sling, hitting the giant Goliath in the center of the forehead, and killing him. When the goal revolves around the Creator of All, the focus becomes larger and larger. A new paradigm must be created by humanity to stop the control enshrouding the world.

In today's world, most humans have a limited understanding of God how language cannot explain what the Creator is, and how the Universe continues to expand into infinity. Our limited minds can't even begin to understand the concept of a ubiquitous Creator.

God, therefore, is first of all a Creator, not of one physical universe but of an infinite variety of probable existences, far more vast than those aspects of the physical universe with which your scientists are familiar. He did not simply send a son to live and die on one small planet. He is a part of all probabilities.

For example: There was no beginning, and there will be no end, yet parables have been given telling you of beginnings and endings simply because with your distorted ideas of time, beginnings and endings seem to be inseparable, valid events. Multidimensional awareness is available to you in your dreams, however, in some trance states, and often even beneath ordinary consciousness as you go about your day. God does not exist apart from or separate from physical reality but exists within it and as a part of it, as he exists within and as a part of all other systems of existence.

Now: God is more than the sum of all the probable systems of reality he (God is androgenous) has created, and yet he is within each one of these without exception. He is therefore within each man and woman. He is also within each spider, shadow, and frog, and this is what man does not like to admit.

"Before the beginning of any war, subconsciously each individual knows not only that a war will occur, but its precise outcome. Battles, like other physical acts, exist first in the mental realm. When this realm is peaceful, there are no wars. All of your physical activities, from the political to the economic and the most insignificant individual concerns, have their origin in mental existence, and their outcome is known.

"To create a harmonious inner existence is a positive act with far-reaching effects and not an act of isolation. To desire peace strongly is to help achieve it. To accept war helps prolong its physical existence.

"These are not idle words, nor are they meant symbolically...That which is feared is feared so strongly and concentrated upon so intensely that it is attracted rather than repelled. The approach should not be fear of war but love of peace; not fear of poverty, but concentration upon the unlimited supplies available on your earth. Desire attracts but fear also attracts. Severe fear is highly dangerous in this respect." From the The Early Sessions, Seth Book 8, Session 337.

Remember that time is an illusion, even in this three-dimensional world, and the future is only a system of probabilities. There is a parallel world where World War III happened but won't take place in our reality. Together we can make monumental changes now that will alter the future. The future is not set in stone.

In the book, *Only Love is Real,* Dr. Brian Weiss was given these words by the Masters: "We choose when we will come into our physical state and when we will leave. We know when we have accomplished what we were sent down here to accomplish. We know when the time is up, and you will accept your death. For you know that you can get nothing more out of this lifetime. When you have time, when you have had the time to rest and re-energize your soul, you are allowed to choose your re-entry back into the physical state. Those people who hesitate, who are not sure of their return here, might lose the chance that was given to them, a chance to fulfill what they must when they're in a physical state."

All of you magnificent beings are here at this time in history for a mission. Trust what God has in store for you. Send out prayers of compassion and love for the suffering, the conflicted, the angry, the sick, those caught in wars, the starving, the murderers, and the criminals. Prayers are powerful thoughts that can heal.

Judge not, lest ye be judged! You may have experienced a similar situation in a past life or perhaps in a future lifetime!

BIBLIOGRAPHY

Bledsoe, Chris, *UFO of God,* self-published on Amazon 2023.

Fowler, Raymond, *The Watchers*, New York: *Bantam Books,* 1991, *The Watchers II*, Newberg, OR: *Wildflower Press*, 1995.

Fuller, John, *Interrupted Journey: Two lost hours aboard a UFO—the abduction of Betty and Barney Hill*, Vintage reprint May 10, 2022.

Luzzatto, Rabbi Moshe Chaim, *The Way of God*, Philipp Feldheim; 5th edition (November 1, 1981).

O'Brien, Cathy, *Trance Formation of America,* Reality Marketing, incorporated; revised edition (September 1, 1995).

Roberts, Jane, *Seth Book 8, The Early Sessions.* New Awareness Network, inc. (reprint March 21, 2014) from the 1960-1970 sessions.

Roubini, Nouriel, *Mega Threats*, Little Brown & Co. October 2022.

Thompson, Craig, *Blankets,* Drawn, and Quarterly; reprint edition (October 13, 2015).

Twain, Mark, *A Connecticut Yankee in King Arthur's Court*, reprint from 1889 on Amazon.

Uttley, Alison, *A Traveller in Time, NYRB* Kids; Reprint edition (February 11, 2020).

Weiss, Brian, *Through Time into Healing*, Simon and

Schuster 2008, and *Only Love is Real,* Grand Central Publishing; Reprint edition (March 1, 1997)

ABOUT THE AUTHOR

Betsey Lewis is an internationally acclaimed psychic and best-selling author with her yearly prophecy books on Amazon. At the age of eight months old, she and her parents had a UFO encounter on a rural road in Northwestern Idaho late one night as they traveled to Southern Idaho. In 1982, renowned MUFON investigator and best-selling author Ann Druffel hypnotized Betsey and her mother and uncovered the missing two hours from their trip—they were abducted by gray extraterrestrials.

At age seven, Betsey witnessed a UFO hovering above her while walking home from her elementary school. Shortly after her UFO encounters, and missing time, she began to dream of catastrophic Earth changes. Betsey has investigated alien abductions stories, UFO sightings, ancient archaeological sites in Louisiana, Native American petroglyph sites in the Northwest, and conducted field investigations into the bizarre cattle mutilations throughout the Northwest during the late 1970s, collaborating with Tom Adams, author of the *Stigmata Report* and renowned cattle mutilation investigator.

Betsey studied indigenous spirituality with Oglala Sioux ceremonial leader Eagle Man and Spiritual Leader of the Western Shoshone Nation, Corbin Harney during the 1990s.

Betsey's guest interviews include Coast-to-Coast AM, Ground Zero with Clyde Lewis, KTalk's Fringe Radio, Fade to Black, WGSO AM in New Orleans, and other well-known shows. She was a keynote speaker at the Alamo/Las Vegas UFO Conference in 2013, and a keynote speaker at the UFO Conference in Albuquerque, New Mexico in 2017. She has authored eighteen non-fiction Amazon books and three fictional children's books available on Amazon.

To learn more about Betsey, her books, upcoming events, and her daily Earth News blog visit **www.betseylewis.com**

Made in the USA
Las Vegas, NV
06 January 2024

84005569R00115